MOTORBOOKS
PowerTech Series ™

PERFORMANCE WELDING

RICHARD FINCH

First published in 1997 by MBI Publishing Company,
729 Prospect Avenue, PO Box 1, Osceola, WI 54020-0001 USA

MBI Publishing Company books are also available at discounts in bulk quantity for industrial or sales-promotional use. For details write to Special Sales Manager at Motorbooks International Wholesalers & Distributors, 729 Prospect Avenue, PO Box 1, Osceola, WI 54020-0001 USA.

Library of Congress Cataloging-in-Publication Data

Finch, Richard.
    Performance welding/Richard Finch.
        p. cm.—(PowerTech)
    Includes index.
    ISBN 0-7603-0393-2 (pbk.: alk. paper)
    1. Automobiles, Racing—Welding. 2. Airplanes—Welding.
3. Welding—Quality control. I. Title. II. Series: MBI Publishing Company powertech series.
TL278.F55   1997
629.28'78—dc21   97-841

On the front cover: Say the word "welding" and most people envision a fully protected person creating an intense light with lots of sparks and smoke. MIG (wire-feed) welding produces effects like this, but TIG (heliarc) and OFW (gas) welding do not. This book explains the differences and teaches you how to become an expert welder in all three processes. *Cover photo courtesy of Sellstrom Manufacturing Corporation*

Designed by Rebecca Allen

Printed in the United States of America

CONTENTS

PREFACE

I thank the following people for their contributions to this book:

Seth and Tannis Hammond of Specialty Welding of Goleta, CA; Tom Giffen and Ron Chase of Western Welding, Goleta, CA; Michael Reitman of the United States Welding Corporation Carson City, NV; Lisa West of the Smiths Equipment Company of Watertown, SD; Dick Casperson of the Miller Electric Company Appleton, WI; Ed Morgan of the Lincoln Electric Company Santa Fe Springs, CA; Hal Olcott of the Victor Equipment Company Denton, TX; Jess Meyers of Belted Air Power, Las Vegas, NV;. Ron Butler of Butler Race Cars, Goleta, CA; Vacuum Atmospheres Company, Mittler Bros Tools, the Wag-Aero Group, Rans Inc., Pro Tools, ESAB, and Laurie Longanecker of B&R Secretarial Services, Goleta, CA.

—Richard Finch

INTRODUCTION

This book will not explain stick welding or any of the welding processes that are usually associated with bridge building, trailer fabrication, and sky-scraper building. That kind of welding has its place in the world, and we all surely depend on welders who assemble those things for us. But there are already a number of books that describe heavy-duty welding.

I wrote *Performance Welding* because existing books on welding could be confusing if you were only interested in building or repairing an airplane or an Indy-type race car. Even the previous books that I have written about welding, by necessity, contained information and instruction about all types of welding and cutting processes, and that could confuse the person who is seeking only the highest quality welding processes.

Therefore, a book was needed that left out all the other welding and cutting processes and concentrated on explaining how to correctly weld lightweight, high-technology structures on aircraft and race cars. That is what this book does.

Obsolete Information

In reviewing several other books that gave instruction in aircraft-quality welding, it was interesting to note that most of the chapters and reprints of articles used in those books were copyrighted or published in the 1930s and occasionally in the late 1950s. If you think about it for a minute, you will immediately realize that airplanes and race cars have changed dramatically since 1935. Technology has made major leaps in more modern processes in almost all areas of transportation and in sports. Metallurgy has made major leaps in strength, materials, and fatigue resistance since the 1930s.

If you were to buy a book this year, only to find that you were buying information that is 30 to 60 years behind the times, you would realize that you are not going to be able to weld things that are current technology.

The Federal Aviation Administration (FAA) recently asked me to update *43.13A, Acceptable Methods, Techniques, and Practices, Aircraft Inspection and Repair,* published in 1972 by the Department of Transportation. This is the standard repair guide that all airframe and power-plant mechanics are directed to use when making repairs on all nonpressurized airplanes. I accepted the challenge and updated the welding chapter in that official guide book.

The interesting thing I found in the 1972 edition was that all the welding repair procedures were for airplanes built before World War II! Even the official government repair procedures were really behind the times. It is okay to repair a 1935 airplane or race car with 1935 procedures, but if you are working with a late 1990s airplane or race car, you need to know how to properly apply the procedures and materials that will make your repairs state-of-the-art.

And if you are building a new structure airplane or race car, you need to take full advantage of the most current and up-to-date welding procedures.

This book will teach you the very latest procedures in TIG (Tungsten Inert Gas) welding, MIG (Metal Inert Gas) welding, and OFW (Oxy-Fuel Welding), and it will tell you about the major advances that have been made in the filler metals (welding rod and wire) in recent years.

Aircraft Factories

There are still aircraft factories that crank out many airplanes every year, using obsolete welding procedures and obsolete welding materials. Why? It's because the FAA has not specified any certain welding procedures that *must* be followed in building new certified airplanes.

The FAA certification procedures presently allow any welding process to be used and any filler material to be used as long as the structure will pass the ± 3 gs or ± 9 gs static test, whichever the aircraft is to be certified to. Then the FAA wants the factory to write maintenance manuals that describe how to repair welds that inevitably crack! If there was a good specification to begin with, the cracks wouldn't appear.

Race Car Factories

Most, but not all, of the Indy race car teams use the best welding rod and the latest welding equipment available. In the *Indy Car Rule Book,* certain types of welding repairs are restricted, as are certain types of chassis and suspension member construction. For instance, in the early 1970s, there were many racing accidents caused by cracked suspension castings. As a result, castings were banned from race car suspension members. Only forged or welded suspension members were allowed. The race car industry was actually ahead of the aircraft industry in metallurgy and welding technology, and still is, in many instances.

Old Rumors

For many years, word-of-mouth advice has been passed on to younger welders by people who had been educated verbally by yet other people in word-of-mouth fashion. Much of this handed-down information has been erroneous.

Things such as postwelding stress relieving by using an oxyacetylene torch, preheating or not preheating, the use of scrap wire to weld with, and other procedures that had no scientific basis were erroneously passed on to newer welders. In this book the metallurgical facts about these old rumors will be described. The end result is that you will be able to accomplish high-quality welding on aerospace materials, and your welds won't break! Now, let's explore the three aircraft-quality welding processes.

CONTENTS

CHAPTER ONE

COMPARING WELDING PROCESSES: TIG, MIG, & GAS

The first welding process used in building airplanes was the oxy-acetylene gas process. In the early 1930s, many airplanes were assembled by gas welding mild steel tubing together to form airplane structures.

In my book collection, I have a reprint of a 1932 airplane builders' handbook that specifies gas welding SAE 1025 thin-wall steel tubing to build airplane fuselages. Most of the mild steel tubing that was specified for building airplanes was 3/4-inch and 1/2-inch diameter by .035-inch wall thickness. Chrome moly 4130 steel tubing did not become generally available to home builders until several years after World War II.

Heliarc welding came next, in the mid- to late 1950s. But heliarc welding equipment was relatively expensive and very bulky at first. When I

first began heliarc welding airplane parts at the Aerostar factory, I used one of those big, heavy, chunky-but-powerful welding machines that was probably manufactured in 1955.

Wire-feed welding, now called MIG welding, first became popular for heavy-duty welding in the auto industry, when the manufacturer used this process to mass-produce car and truck frames. My first experience with MIG welding came in late 1958 when I began building racing go-karts by wire-feed welding the frames. In this chapter I will explain the processes to help you decide which welding process best suits your finances and intended use.

TIG Welding

In TIG welding, a high-temperature confined arc is formed that heats

TIG welding is the easiest, cleanest, and most precise of all manual welding methods. Here I am TIG tack-welding a towbar bracket for one of my airplane projects, using a modular MIG-TIG welder.

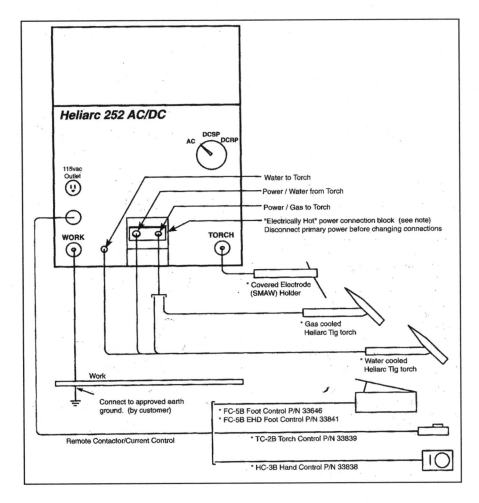

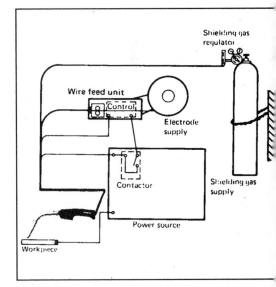

The only company that can legally call its TIG welders "Heliarc" machines is ESAB of Florence, South Carolina. In this illustration, you can see the schematic of a TIG-welding setup. *ESAB Welding and Cutting Products*

Typical MIG or wire-feed welding setups require these basic elements for operation. *Lincoln Electric Company*

the base metal to the melting point for the purpose of fusion welding.

TIG welding uses less heat to join metal than either MIG or gas welding and is by far the most controllable of all manual (not automatic) welding processes. It is so accurate that you could weld a thin piece of .010-inch steel sheet to a thick piece of 6-inch steel billet and not burn through the thin sheet, yet get good penetration into the thick billet.

In fact, TIG welding allows for fusion welding without the addition of filler rod, making it possible to produce welds without extra weld seam build-up. And with a foot pedal amp control, or a thumb amp control on the TIG torch, you can actually strike an arc, start a tiny weld puddle, and without moving the puddle or adding welding rod, maintain the same molten weld puddle for minutes or even hours at a time. That is how controllable TIG welding is.

The advantage to this precise puddle control is that it provides adequate time to properly add filler rod material

to the puddle. You can strike an arc, form a puddle, then carefully and accurately add just the right amount of filler rod at exactly the right place in the molten weld puddle.

MIG Welding

MIG welding, commonly called wire-feed welding because a thin wire is fed into the weld puddle by an electric motor drive system, is quickly gaining in popularity because it is easy to operate and is a relatively fast process. A TIG welder can weld about 6 inches of .050-inch steel sheet in one minute, whereas a MIG welder can weld up to 24 inches of the same material in one minute.

There are pros and cons to MIG welding the more exotic thin-wall 4130 steel tubes and thin sheets of 4130 steel used in aircraft construction. Here are some of the considerations:

Pros of MIG Welding

It is easy to turn the power switch on, turn the gas on, and merely point the gun and pull the trigger to wire-

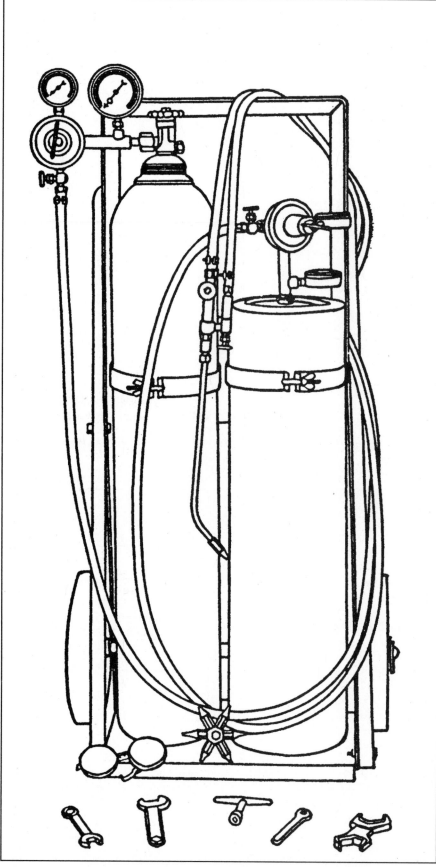

Gas-welding setups have not changed much since the early years. This is a typical commercial oxyacetylene welding rig used in the 1930s.

feed weld race car frames and aircraft fuselage structures. It is also possible to weld a lot more inches of weld bead per hour with MIG welding than with any other welding process. This is because the welding filler metal is fed from a spool of wire that can be fed into the weld continuously for as long as the welder holds the trigger down on the welding gun.

Usually, the MIG weld bead is a very sound weld, almost as sound as a perfectly done TIG weld. Once the amps, volts, and wire-feed speed are properly adjusted, MIG welding is a very high-quality welding process.

Cons of MIG Welding

Several problems associated with MIG welding include the normal tendency of an electrode-fed arc weld to start off cold. That means that each start of the arc is not fully penetrated for the first fractions of an inch of weld bead. Once the MIG weld bead is established, the heat and penetration is normal, but it always starts off cold.

Another disadvantage to MIG welding is that the process is highly intolerant of any gaps in the fit-up of the parts. Usually, the MIG wire is .025 inch to .030 inch in diameter, and if there is a gap of more than the diameter of the electrode, the wire can slip into the crack and not make a weld bead. Another disadvantage of welding small-diameter thin-wall tubing with MIG is that once you accidentally burn a hole in the tubing, it is very hard to fill the hole without stopping to make a patch for it, or there will be times you will have to use gas welding to patch holes made by MIG welding.

And likely the primary difficulty with MIG welding is that once you squeeze the trigger on the MIG gun, you are committed to move right along with making a weld bead, ready or not. If you make a bad start, sometimes you have to stop, grind or cut out the beadweld, and then start over again.

Gas Welding

The oldest aircraft welding process—gas (oxyacetylene) welding—is still a good, dependable process. Oxyacetylene welding is very much the same process that it was in 1920. The two gases, oxygen and the

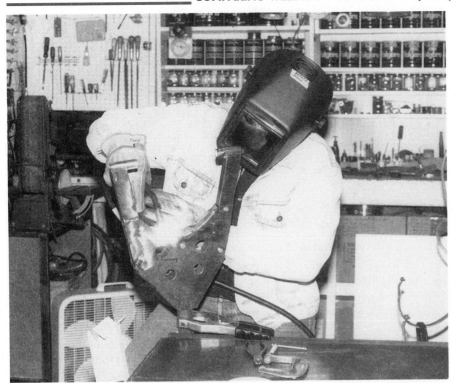

MIG welding with a 75 percent/25 percent CO_2/argon gas outer shield is the fastest but less accurate of all manual welding processes.

Gas welding (oxyacetylene gas), as I am demonstrating, is a relatively clean and dependable metal-joining process, although it is less accurate than TIG welding. However, gas welding is far less expensive than most other welding processes.

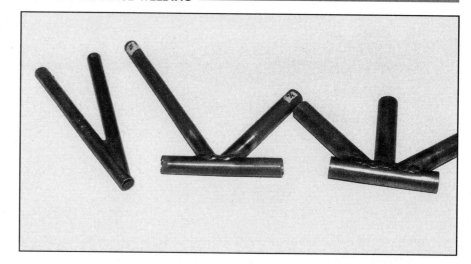

From left to right, these aircraft grade 4130 tube assemblies were welded by TIG, MIG, and gas. TIG is more accurate and clean. MIG is fast and less accurate. Gas is slow and somewhat less accurate, but reasonably priced.

fuel gas acetylene, are still the same as they have been for 100 years or more. The gas welding torches have slowly evolved to the point at which they are at today, but a torch made 50 years ago would still be a dependable aircraft welding torch.

Gas welding rigs are still the least expensive of all welding setups, too. Chapter 2 will explain the best ones to have.

The neutral flame (equal pressure of oxygen and acetylene) combines to produce a flame temperature

at the inner core of about 5,000 degrees F, a temperature that is also used in TIG welding. The difference is that the oxyacetylene flame produces fewer BTUs (units of heat), and it produces much more heat of a lower temperature at its outer flame.

Michael Andretti's back-up Indy race car makes use of TIG welding in the very delicate but strong front suspension. Most of the welding on his car was made by the TIG process.

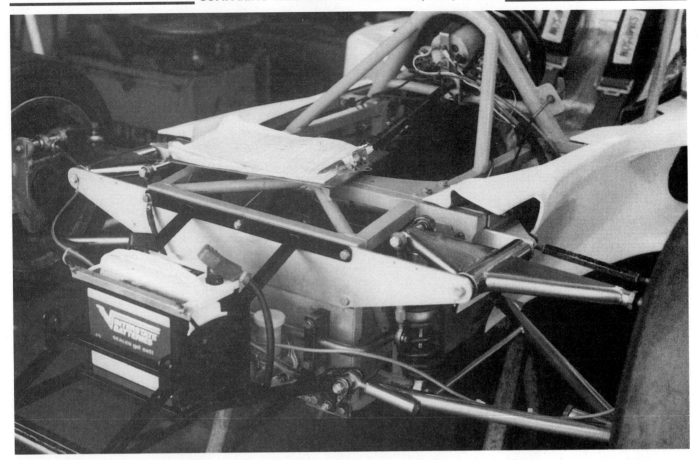

Most of the frame and lightweight fabricated front suspension on this Jim Russell Driving School Formula Ford car is TIG-welded for strength and neatness.

Left
In the left of this picture you can see the TIG-welded aluminum radiator filler tank on this Buick V-6 Indy Lights race car. The TIG-welded exhaust system is complicated, but it is actually easy to fabricate by proper fitting and TIG welding.

I TIG welded both engine mounts, all the turbocharger brackets, the stainless steel exhaust waste gates, the aluminum air boxes, and the gas heater exhaust on this Aerostar S/N266. I also MIG welded all six seat frames. Silver solder was used to make strong electrical connections at the rear-mounted dual 12-volt batteries.

What this means is that in the process of welding a butt joint of thin-wall tubing, the heat-affected area of the tube will be several times larger with gas welding than with TIG or MIG welding. But that is seldom a problem. The nature of the gas welding flame does heat the assembly up more, but in steel and aluminum thicknesses of less than .100 inch, the gas welding torch is very adequate.

There are a few difficulties with gas welding. When you are attempting to weld inside corners, the flame is blown back toward you, and that makes the heat on your hands uncomfortable. Another difficulty is

Bellanca Viking airplanes, from the mid-1970s on, featured MIG-welded fuselages, tail structures, and landing gear assemblies. Prior to about 1975, they were welded by TIG and gas processes.

in welding next to an edge of tubing or plate. The heat of the torch is considerably more broad than TIG or MIG welding, and this causes sharp edges to want to melt away. The solution to that problem is to add extra length to the metal joint to be welded and then trim it to the correct size after the weld is completed.

Race Car Welding

Race car fabricators rely on TIG welding almost exclusively in the construction of Formula I, Indy cars, Indy Lights, and the smaller formula cars such as Formula Ford and Super Vee classes.

The reason for this is the relatively small number of cars built in each of these classes. TIG welding is the most accurate of all welding processes, and with fewer cars to build, it does not matter so much that it takes a little longer to fabricate suspension and systems parts.

In this chapter, look at the photographs of Michael Andretti's back-up Indy race car front suspension. It is made from 4130 steel tubing that has threaded inserts TIG welded in each end. MIG welding would not

This close-up picture of the Bellanca Citabria door frame shows the welding detail of the MIG-welded tubular structure, the door hinge plates, and finger doublers that make this a very strong airplane fuselage.

be adequate for those spindly looking suspension tubes, because MIG welding cannot be controlled accurately enough to make 100 percent sound welds.

In the Jim Russell Formula Ford race car pictures in this chapter, note the smooth, accurate TIG welds in the frame and the suspension. Again, MIG would have been less adequate

Bellanca Citabria aerobatic airplanes feature MIG-welded 4130 steel tube fuselage and tail structures. A completed Citabria is in the background.

The fiberglass fuselage Glastar experimental airplane actually employs riveted aluminum wings and tail. A MIG- and TIG-welded 4130 steel tube structural frame is under the fiberglass skin of the fuselage.

My VW Scirocco class SSB race car complied with SCCA racing rules with the addition of a TIG-welded roll cage, TIG-welded window net brackets, and TIG-welded 5-point seat belt restraint brackets.

here because of the need for 100-percent accurate welds. And in the pictures of the Buick V-6 Indy Lights radiator installation, it is easy to see that gas welding or MIG welding those parts would not have been easy or sound, if possible at all.

Aircraft MIG Welding

Many aircraft fuselages have been MIG welded in the past 25 or 30 years. Obviously, this welding process works, and there have been little or no problems with airplanes or components welded by this process.

Although it may seem that the inherent need to start welding cold and to weld a steady, straight bead would be a problem in small-diameter, round thin-wall tubing, there are several solutions, which I'll explain in Chapter 7. Often, the production quantity demands require faster methods, as is possible with MIG welding.

Race Car MIG Welding

A number of racing classes depend on a few constructors to build

Most of the frame welding on this ARS race car is by the MIG process.

relatively large numbers of race car rolling chassis. The requirements to provide dozens of tube-frame race car chassis dictate that the very fastest fabrication methods be used, and MIG welding fills that dictate.

Gas Welding Airplanes

For low-production airplane fuselage construction, a good quality oxyacetylene welding rig is very adequate. In sheer numbers, the large amount of certified airplanes still flying 50 to 75 years after being welded with gas is a strong statement in favor of gas welding as a good, safe welding process.

There are many airplane designs available today that depend on gas welding to assemble rudder pedal assemblies, engine mounts, and complete fuselage assemblies. When properly performed, gas welding is perfectly adequate, and it is easy to do properly. Read more in Chapters 9 and 10 about gas welding.

Upper right
Stick (arc) welding was used to attach the brake drum backing plate adapter ring to the axle on this 1938 Army Air Force training airplane wheel assembly. Arc welding is obsolete for aircraft assembly since MIG and TIG processes were invented in 1955 and 1945, respectively.

Lower right
This World War II observation airplane axle assembly was fabricated by gas welding; however, this process is still viable and structurally adequate for similar aircraft.

Tent sales like this one at welding supply outlets are good places to find sale prices on welding supplies and to try out the newest equipment.

CHAPTER TWO

SHOPPING FOR WELDING EQUIPMENT

My first welding rig was a very used $50 Victor Aircrafter set with torch, regulators, hoses, and tips. After putting in $2 worth of new O-rings in the torch, it welded my go-karts and SCCA race cars just fine. I do know that I sure did get my investment back on that torch.

My first Heliarc™ welder was an antique that must have been one of the first ones ever made. It served me well in building over 200 airplane engine mounts in a period of just over one year.

You can calculate your budget and go shopping for your welding equipment, but you should know up front that there are cheap welders sold by stores that can't even tell you how to use them. You can buy arc welders for less than $100 and MIG welders for less than $200 and I'll tell you that these welders could turn you against welding pretty fast! I have seen several of these machines and have tried them out, and they will make you think that welding is an art you can't master. You're better off leaving them at the store where you found them. If

you did accidentally buy one, it is extremely unlikely that you will ever find repair parts for it, and it is highly unlikely that you will even get it to work the way it was advertised to work. But don't despair! This book will help you get the most out of whatever welding equipment you may have.

In this chapter I will tell you about your choices and make suggestions about where to look for equipment.

Mail-Order Welders

Two of my gas welding outfits came from mail-order dealers, and they both work okay. One gas welder was advertised as working *almost* as well as a TIG welder, but it really doesn't. I didn't expect it to, so I am not disappointed. But if I had expected it to be as advertised, I would have returned it for a refund. The lesson here is to make sure you can return *any* piece of welding equipment if it will not perform as advertised. But don't wait too long to request a return. Companies frown on people who buy equipment for a project, use it, then ask for refunds.

Used Welders

One local college recently shut down its entire machine shop program and sold all the machinery at 10 percent of acquisition cost. A very large aviation corporation in this same area recently went out of business, and it sold everything, including several high-quality TIG welders, at an auction. They sold for 10 percent to 20 percent of original acquisition cost. Good quality, name-brand welding equipment should last for 50 years or more if it is properly maintained. Consider buying used equipment if your budget is low.

New Technology

We are all familiar with the recent major improvements in the electronics industry, including portable telephones, computers, and home electronics. The same technology has engulfed the welding industry, and you need to know where to go to find out about the very latest in welding technology. And believe it or not, tent sales are often on the cutting edge.

Last year at a tent sale in the Los Angeles area, I discovered a new, lightweight square-wave TIG and stick welder that would be perfect for small shops, home shops, and for a portable welder in a big shop. It was so new that the few handout brochures about the new welder were photocopies that had pencil-marked changes. Now, about six months later, I have just seen the first full-page color ad for that welder in a monthly magazine. Tent sales are great places to see new technology *and* to get bargains on great name-brand welding equipment. Tent sales are usually held in parking lots of established welding supply businesses.

Square-Wave Technology

Just like in the computer industry, electronics have progressed in welding equipment, making possible superior characteristics that provide a very smooth output welding arc in the AC aluminum and magnesium welding mode. Square-wave technology also smoothes out the DC welding output when welding steel, stainless steel, and titanium. Take the author's advice and do not buy any new TIG or MIG welding machine until you have compared square-wave technology with

You can buy a good, dependable TIG-stick welder like this one at company closings and school close-out sales. This Lincoln Idealarc is a very good TIG welder, but without the newer square-wave features. Usual price is $200 to $400 used.

the original AC/DC equipment. My guess is that you will elect to go with a square-wave welder. All of the name-brand welder companies now manufacture these machines.

Name Brands

In the 10 years since my first welding book was written, at least half the companies listed in that book sold out and merged with other companies, often forming brand-new companies with new names. The same phenomenon is still happening today. Literally, as this chapter is being written, two longtime, well-known welding equipment manufacturers, Miller Electric Manufacturing Company and Hobart Brothers Company, merged under the management of Illinois Tool Works. Also under the same management are PowCon,

One of the newer square-wave AC/DC TIG and SAW (stick) welding machines is this 175-pound, 175-amp Lincoln square-wave welder that sells for $1,300 complete with all accessories except a cart and an argon bottle.

Oxo, Tri Mark, Corex, and McKay, other longtime companies in the welding business.

Therefore, it is wise for anyone who plans to stay current in the welding field to visit American Welding Society meetings, visit your local welding trade schools, and attend at least two or three welding trade shows every year.

Portable Rigs

The days of trailer- or truck-mounted portable welding rigs is becoming a thing of the past. New inverter technology makes it possible to have a pipe-welding-capacity power supply that you can carry in the trunk of your car and is not much larger than your arc welding helmet. Though at this time, none of the inverter welders will weld aluminum

or magnesium; you can expect that to change soon.

Modular Add-Ons

For about half the price of the lowest-cost TIG welder, you can purchase a modular TIG add-on that features capacitor start or, in some products, high-frequency start (preferable). This means that if you have a "good old" stick welder or a "good old" wire feed welder, you can use its transformer to power a TIG torch, even with a foot pedal control and argon gas timing.

Electronic Helmets

For many years, welders who did stick welding, TIG welding, and MIG welding were forced to aim the torch, stick, or gun at the weld with their helmets up, then shake their head to

lower their helmet, and hope their aim at the weld joint had not moved. This problem was the biggest obstacle to learning to weld quickly. Even us old-timers never really mastered the "flip-the-helmet-down" trick. And we always had to stop welding, raise the helmet, and look to see if we had made a good weld.

Very recently some savvy engineer invented an electronic welding lens that is a shade 3 (sunglasses shade) when no welding arc is present, and it changes to a shade 10, 11, or 12 as soon as an arc is struck. The change is not instant. You do see the arc, but only for about 1/500 to 1/125,000 of a second. What this means is that at the end of a long day of arc welding, your eyes will itch about the same as if you had spent the day at the beach without sunglasses.

Tim Marr of Lincoln Electric Company proudly shows a top-of-the-line Lincoln square-wave 355-amp TIG and stick welder that has numerous extra features. This machine sells for $3,600 less cart, cooler, argon cylinders, making the cost for a complete unit about $4,500.

Upper left
The next step up in TIG welders is this electronic control panel Lincoln Square Wave TIG 255-amp welding machine. Complete, as shown here with a closed-loop radiator and two argon bottles, expect to spend about $3,500.

Lower left
The dream of many home shop welders, as well as portable weld rigs, is this Thermaldynamics 190-amp TIG welder that runs off 110-volt house current or 220-volt shop current. It is a DC-only welder that sells for about $1,500, but it only weighs 19 pounds!

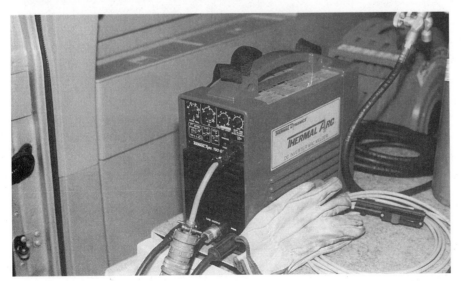

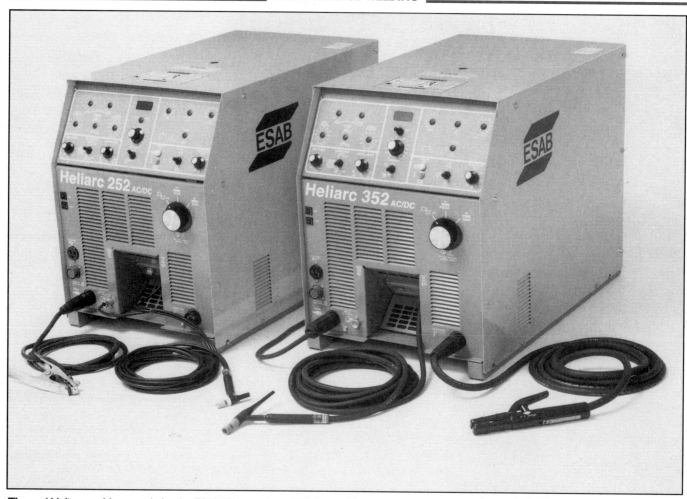

The *real* Heliarc welders, made by the ESAB Corporation of Florence, South Carolina. These 252-amp and 352-amp TIG and stick welders also feature square-wave technology. *ESAB Welding and Cutting Products*

Modular TIG adapters, such as this MTA160 sold by Daytona MIG, make it possible to use the transformer from a MIG welder or a DC-only stick welder to have TIG capabilities at a cost of less than $1,000 including torch and foot pedal.

Daytona MIG Company specializes in mail-order sales of this Pocket Pulse TIG DC-only welder and the 110-volt Pocket Plasma Cutter. They are nice for small shop use or as backup machines in larger fabrication shops.

Upper left
This 220-volt Pocket Pulse TIG machine is made in Italy and sold by Daytona MIG Company through ads in car magazines.

Lower left
Electronic welding helmets let the welder see the TIG, MIG, or stick at a sunglasses #3 tint before striking the arc; they change to #10, 11, or 12 lens tint within 1/100,000 of a second after the arc is started. They cost between $125 and $350.

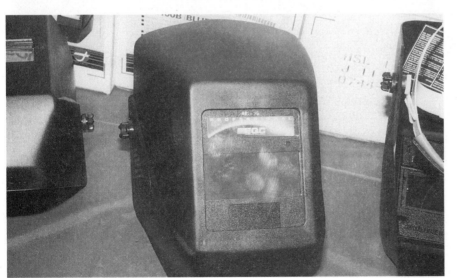

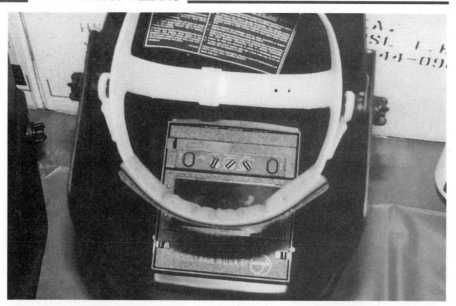

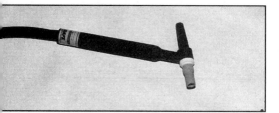

My favorite size TIG torch is this Weldcraft WP-10 torch with a short back cap. This water-cooled torch will weld up to 1/4-inch-thick aluminum and steel.

The back side of the Jackson electronic welding helmet shows the five buttons that adjust the shades this helmet will operate at.

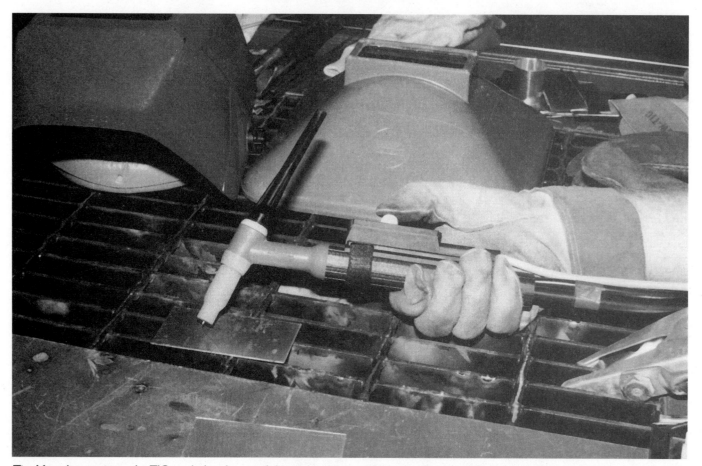

Tim Marr demonstrates the TIG torch thumb control that starts and stops this large water-cooled torch without the need for a foot control. You cannot operate a TIG foot control when you are on your knees trying to weld something 1 foot off the floor.

Every TIG welder needs to ask Santa Claus to bring him or her one of these TIG Cradles made by the Raterman Manufacturing Company of Santa Clara, California. It conveniently holds all the TIG parts a welder needs!

This lens is a definite improvement over the old-style helmet.

These helmets start at $100 and cost up to $275 or more. They really do contribute to much more accurate arc starts in stick, TIG, and MIG welding, as well as plasma arc cutting.

TIG Torches

Like ballpoint pens, TIG torches come in many sizes and qualities. For most aircraft welding, a small water-cooled torch is best. When shopping for a water-cooled torch, try to find one that can be adapted to gas lens operation. There are several good brands of TIG torches on the market, and the way to shop for a torch is to ask to see a selection of collets, chucks, and cups for the particular torch you are interested in. If you can buy a full range of collets from 0.020-inch up to 5/32 inch, then you can expect good service from that torch. If

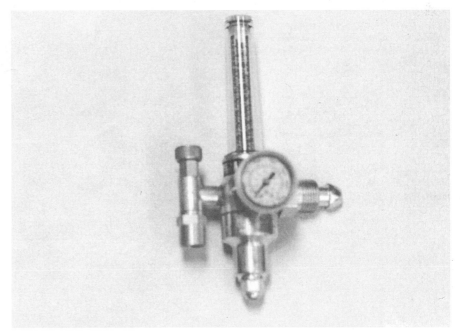

An often-forgotten accessory for a TIG welder is a second argon flowmeter for back-gas purging stainless steel and titanium welds.

This heavy-duty TIG or MIG torch water pump pays for itself in recirculating cooling water rather than letting the water go down the drain.

Right
Miller Electric Company of Appleton, Wisconsin, makes this closed-circuit coolant radiator for TIG and MIG water-cooled torches.

Miller Electric Company sells this 150-pound Econotig welder that does AC/DC TIG welds as well as stick welds.

parts are not available, don't even think about buying it.

Thumb Controls

You will not always be able to TIG weld at table top level. There will come a day when the weld must be reached by standing on a ladder, or when the weld is 6 inches off the floor. For many years, the solution to those hard-to-reach TIG welds was to lay a brick on the foot pedal and hope for the right amount of heat from the torch, or go find a helper to push the pedal for you when you said to. Welds made this way were never as good as they could be.

The solution to that TIG welding problem is to buy a thumb- or forefinger-operated TIG amp control switch that you attach to your TIG torch. You won't use the thumb or finger control TIG switch much, but when you do need it, you will be happy that you have it.

Consumables

Any welding product that is normally used up in welding is called a consumable. This includes welding and brazing rod, wire on spools, flux for brazing, solder, pastes for soldering, and even MIG gun parts, plasma cutter parts, and TIG cups and tungsten. Chapter 12 covers these items.

Extra Flowmeter

For less than $90 you can buy a spare flowmeter for use in making back-gas purges of stainless steel and titanium welds. The price of the extra flowmeter is so low that just one critical weld project will pay for it. This is not a starting kit item because you might weld for many hours before you ever need to back-gas purge something, but when a stainless steel or titanium weld project comes up, by all means invest in a spare flowmeter.

Gas Welders

The best, smoothest, easiest-to-operate gas welding set I have ever used was one that was loaned to me to make a race car repair at Sears Point Raceway at Sonoma, California. I

25

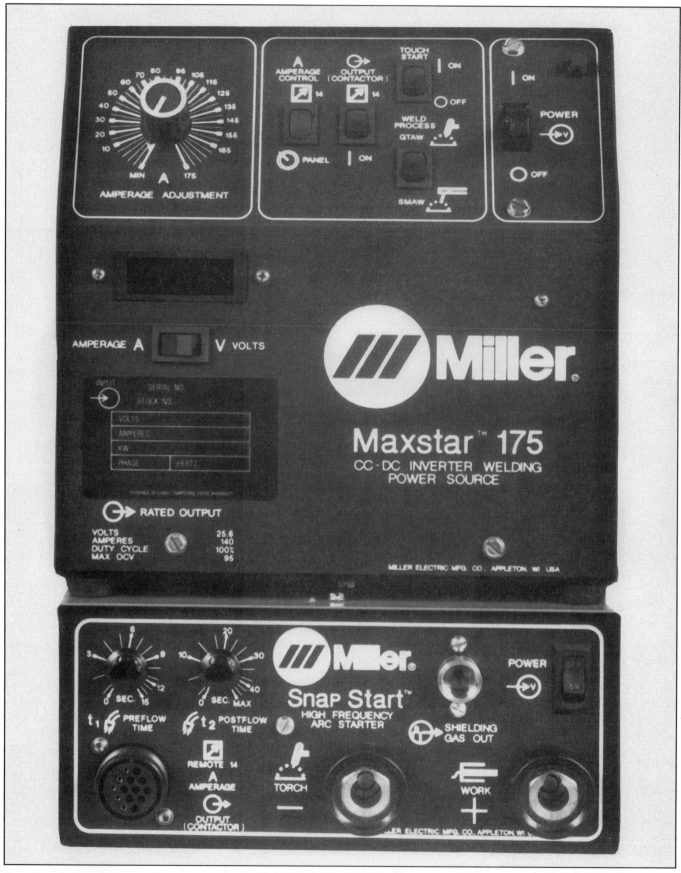

Becoming more popular are these modular units that allow fabrication shops to tailor their welding equipment to the needs of the shop.
Miller Electric Company

For repeatable high-quality TIG, MIG, stick welding, Miller provides a full control panel on this Syncrowave 250 arc welding power source. *Miller Electric Company*

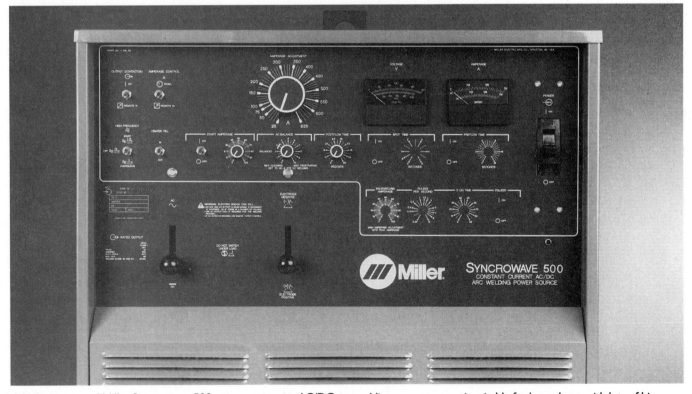

A higher-powered Miller Syncrowave 500 constant-current AC/DC arc welding power source is suitable for large shops with lots of big welding jobs. *Miller Electric Company*

don't recall what brand it was, but that set worked great!

The point to this little story is that superior gas welders do exist. Keep your hopes up, and keep your eyes open for this kind of torch. Do not buy the cheapest discount store or mail-order torch you can find. Instead, go to welding sales. One frequent loss-leader at those tent sales is the small, portable, handy-carried gas welding and cutting rig. But make sure you can buy extra tips and extra rosebud tips for any torch you decide to buy. No spare parts should mean *no sale*! And stick with brand names like Thermadyne (formerly Victor), Lincoln (formerly Harris), and Smiths. Also, you might want to investigate the pistol-grip Dillon/Henrob torch as a second torch.

Shop Tools

Every weld shop must have one or more air-operated cut-off tools and a

This is a high-tech TIG welder that is purported to be able to weld aluminum race car blocks back together with ease. The welder costs $6,000.

small angle sander. Tubing benders are a necessity, and several new models exist today. Many new benders feature hand-operated hydraulic jacks to make smooth, wrinkle-free bends in thin-wall tubing. Most of these tubing benders will be mail-order purchased, and you can find addresses and phone numbers in race car magazines and aircraft builders' magazines.

Plasma Cutters

Any welding shop that uses a TIG or MIG welder for even two hours a day would benefit from a plasma cutter. Shop air-operated plasma cutters are the only efficient way to cut stainless steel of any thickness from .020 inch up to 3/8 inch.

They also cut pencil-thin kerfs in any metal and leave very little dross or slag on the back side of the cut. Any shop that fabricates mild steel or stainless steel exhaust systems absolutely must own a plasma cutter, especially for cutting out 3/16-inch and 1/4-inch flanges for the pipes.

Plasma cutters are available in 110-volt, 220-volt, and 440-volt configurations. Mail-order welding supply companies all feature 110-volt plasma cutters, but some of the bottom-line cutters must be push-started, which is not very useful. Remember this motto: "Try it before you buy it," or make sure you get a satisfaction guarantee.

Retail Welding Stores

Much like car dealerships, service after the welding supply sale is more important than the initial purchase. Shop at least three or four local dealers before you decide where to do business. Retail welding stores vary widely in service even before the sale. Don't fence yourself in to doing business with a bad dealer.

Every welding shop, regardless of size or types of welding, should have one of these portable gas welding/cutting/heating rigs. The total cost of this outfit with two gas bottles and the cart is $395.

Portable plasma cutters are a time- and money-saving investment if your shop spends even two hours a day in metal fabrication. *ESAB Welding and Cutting Products.*

Buy several of these magnetic angle jigs. Once you use one, you will be addicted.

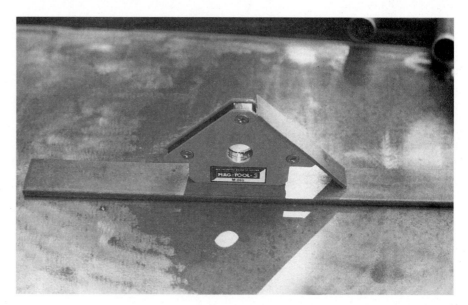

This new, unused air-operated die grinder and cut-off wheel cost $15. Any shop should have one or more of these.

Defective welds are easily cut out with an air-operated die grinder, as the welder is doing here on a Lycoming engine mount. *WAG Aero Group*

CONTENTS

For nearly 75 years, filing fishmouth joints in tubular structures was the best way to ensure a good fit-up. Today, there is a better way to do this task.

CHAPTER THREE

FITTING AND CLEANING

A properly fitted and cleaned weld assembly makes the welding process much easier and more sound than a poorly fitted, dirty assembly. Fitting is the most time-consuming part of welding any assembly, but fitting is also the major contributor to good, high-quality welds.

Several years ago, while working as a nuclear power plant welding inspector, I found that the pipe fitters did about 80 percent of the work and the higher-paid welder did only 20 percent of the work in fabricating the piping in the plant. You will find the same time ratio in fitting and welding aircraft or race car assemblies.

File to Fit

In the many books I have on the subject of pipe and tube welding, many solutions to fishmouthing tubing are described. Some welders actually dress several widths of abrasive grinding wheels to a half-circle and *grind* the fishmouth into each tube end! Others try to band-saw the fishmouth into the tube, then finish the notch with a half-round file. Still others mount a milling cutter in a lathe and push the tube into the cutter (rather dangerous).

Hole Saw

Some clever fabricator designed a hole saw mandrel and an adjustable tubing clamp assembly and revolutionized the fitting of tubing for welding. In the photos in this chapter, you can see how easy it is to cut tubing to the *exact* angle and the *exact* fishmouth size. And the entire process to set up for, say, a 52-degree angle cut in a piece of 1 1/2-inch diameter x 0.95-inch wall thickness tube is about one minute. The actual cut takes even less time.

After the hole-saw fishmouth cut is made, there will be burrs around the saw cut that must be removed with a file or with a sanding belt. Then, the area to be welded must be sanded clean of mill scale and cleaned with acetone before making the weld.

Fitting the Parts Before Welding

The fit-up of tubing or parts to be

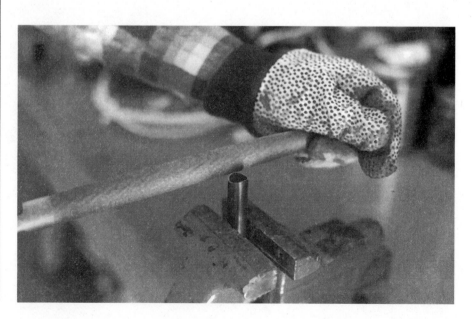

CAUTION

When using a bimetal hole saw to fishmouth steel tubing of less than 1-inch diameter and less than .049-inch wall thickness, be aware of the fact that the coarse hole saw blade teeth can all shatter off if special care is not taken to cut very slowly. By saying this I mean to engage the saw into the tubing very gradually to avoid shattering off all the teeth in the hole saw.

Quite likely, some enterprising manufacturer will see the opportunity to make special bimetal hole saws for cutting thin-wall tubing. Ideally, a 1/2-inch diameter hole saw should have 15 teeth per inch rather than the 6 or 8 teeth per inch that is currently available. Meanwhile, cut small, thin tubes slowly.

Every welding project begins with cutting the materials into the proper lengths. A cut-off saw like the one being used here by Mitch Matthews costs about $200 and will save lots of hacksaw work.

welded is the most essential part of weld preparation. Do a good fit-up and your weld will be much easier to do, and it will be stronger and prettier! Here are a few pointers:

1. Fit every part to have less gap than the thickness of the welding rod being used. In most cases, the gap between aircraft parts to be welded should be less than .020 inch. If the welding rod can be inserted between the parts, the fit-up is less than ideal; it's too loose for a good, strong weld.

2. Wide gaps can be filled, but bridging open air between the parts causes hot spots in the weld, and the air gap on the back side of the weld allows atmospheric contaminants such as hydrogen and oxygen to weaken and crack the weld. These wide gaps in the weld will cause fatigue cracking in the weld at a later time. Hidden hot cracking often occurs in poorly fitted joints.

3. The weld joints will last a lifetime if properly designed and fitted before welding. Take an extra 5 or 10 minutes and fit the joints properly.

4. Tubing joints can be fitted perfectly if you use one of the hole-saw tubing notchers that are on the market. They sell for $149 to $279, and

they can make fitting tubes much easier than filing and grinding each fishmouth by hand.

Clean the Parts Thoroughly Before Welding

1. All new metal will have oil and scale on it. Even 4130 steel, stainless steel, and aluminum will *not* be ready to weld as it comes to you from the supplier. Stainless steel will have oil or protective paper and sticky glue on it. Aluminum will have oil, paper, or aluminum oxide on it, and 4130 Chromemoly steel will have pickling oil and mill scale

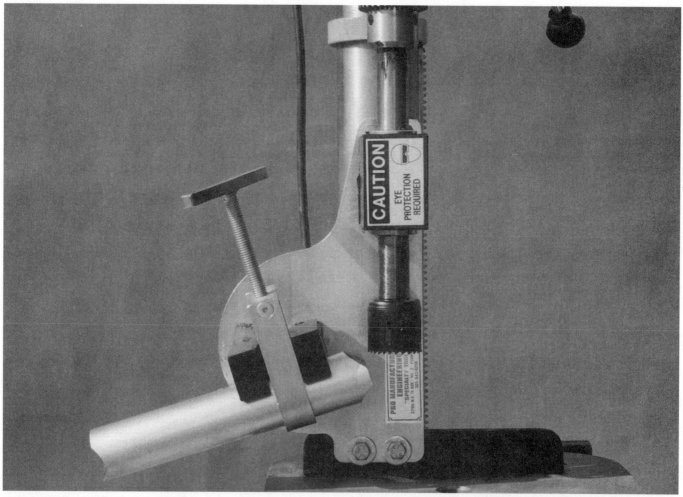

Hole-saw fishmouth tools can accurately make tubular fit-ups in just a fraction of the time it takes to do the same job by hand. *Pro Tools*

I like to mount my Joint Jigger fishmouth tool on my workbench and operate it with a 1/2-inch drill motor. It even notches rectangular tubing.

on it when it comes to you. This "dirt" will contaminate the weld if it is not removed prior to welding.

2. All old, used, repairable metal will have paint, oil, rust, corrosion, and oxidation on it. This "dirt" absolutely must be cleaned off before welding. Again, "dirt" contaminates and weakens welds.

Recommended Cleaning Methods Prior to Welding

1. The gray mill scale on the surface of 4130 Chromemoly steel must be removed, and the metal must be sanded to a bright, new-appearing metal. The mill scale must be cleaned off 1 inch back from the edge to be welded. Tubing can be hand-sanded with strip emery paper of about 80 grit in a manner similar to shining your shoes. You can also use some of the open screen type sanding strips to clean off the mill scale from the tubes. Flat sheets of 4130 steel can be sanded by hand-block sanding from the edges to be welded back a distance of 1 inch. Use a piece of 80-

to 120-grit emery paper wrapped around a block of wood to make the sanding easier.

2. Just a few minutes prior to welding, clean the weld area of the sheet-metal tubes with acetone or denatured alcohol using a clean, white, lint-free cloth to remove all grease and oil from the weld area. Fingerprint oils contaminate welds, too. Clean the parts thoroughly, as if you were going to paint them. Do not expect the heat from welding to evaporate the dirt and oils.

3. Immediately prior to welding, clean the first two or three sticks of welding rod with a clean, lint-free white cloth saturated with acetone or denatured alcohol. From that point, do not touch the welding rod with your bare fingers or with dirty or oily gloves.

Welding Conditions: Where to Do the Welding

1. Do your welding in a clean, warm, well-lighted area that is free of wind and drafts from fans and open

CAUTION

Do not, under any circumstances, sand thin-wall tubing or thin sheet metal with a power sanding belt or disc, since power sanding would remove too much metal and severely weaken the metal in the welded zone. Hand sanding is the only safe way to remove mill scale or oxidation from metal to be welded.

Sandblasting or glass-bead cleaning will safely clean off mill scale or oxidation, but the clean-up process to remove all the sand or glass dust from the part is not worth the time it takes. You absolutely do not want to weld your valuable parts if they are covered with sand dust and glass dust.

Also, do not attempt to remove mill scale or oxidation with a power wire brush because the brush will imbed metal from its bristles into the metal to be welded, and this wire brush metal will contaminate your welds. Also, if the power wire brush is quite stiff, it will actually erode the parts to be welded and cause them to be weakened in the weld zone where you cleaned them.

Every tube must be cleaned before welding. Here I am using a strip of carborundum emery cloth to sand the thin film of mill scale off a 3/4 x .032-inch chromemoly tube. Every place that will be welded must be cleaned like this.

doors and windows. Make sure that there are no liquid or solid combustibles in the welding area that could catch fire from sparks or arcs from your welding.

2. Welding in bright sunlight is far better than welding in a dark room. You can see the weld seam and the weld puddle better under good lighting conditions.

3. Welds made in warm rooms, 80 degrees F to 95 degrees F, are more likely to be good welds than those made in cold rooms. The parts you are welding should never be cold to the touch.

4. If you are welding parts that are 1/4 inch thick, you will have better luck if you preheat the parts to 250

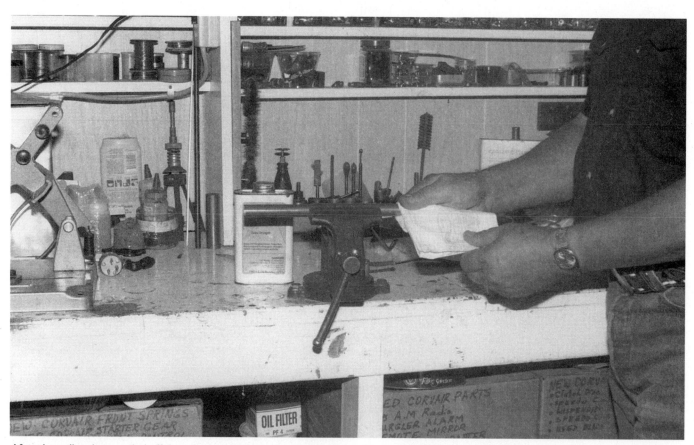

After the mill scale is sanded off the tube, acetone on a paper towel is used to remove all traces of oil and dust before the tube is welded.

These two pieces of 7/8 x .032-inch tube are fitted perfectly and the mill scale has been sanded off. Try to make every tubular joint fit like this.

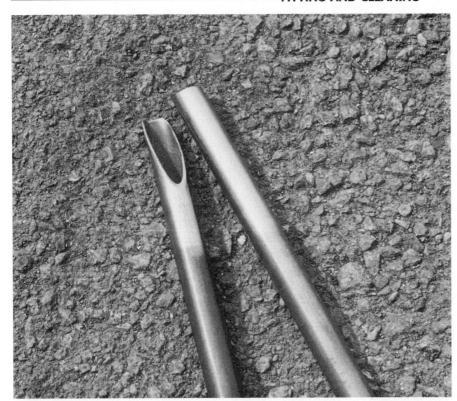

For angles greater than 45 degrees, some hand fitting still has to be done, as is shown on these two tubes for a race car suspension.

The tube that angles up to the right in this picture has been poorly fitted. You can see the large gap that would surely be the cause of a crack in the weld if the tube is not replaced with one that fits properly.

Mittler Brothers Machine makes this heavy-duty tubing notcher that uses a milling cutter to notch the tubes for NASCAR-type roll cages.

You will need to make lots of weld-on tabs like these to attach body panels, wiring harnesses, fuel lines, and many other things to your race car or airplane tubular structure.

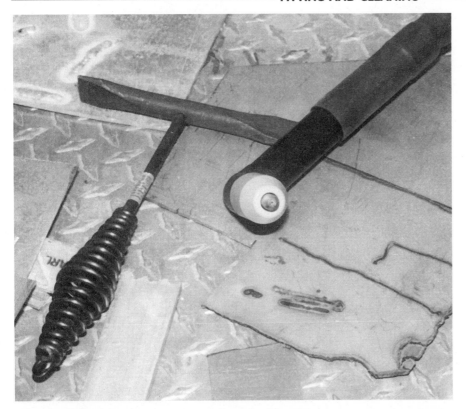

This plasma cutter torch can cut pencil-fine lines in anything that is metallic, including aluminum and stainless steel. It is *the* solution for cutting out stainless steel exhaust flanges from 1/4-inch thick stainless plate.

High-tech airplane fabrication companies now use numerically controlled plasma cutters to precisely trim and fit very small-diameter 4130 steel tubing for use in airplane fuselage structures. *RANS, Inc.*

degrees F, and if the part is thicker, be sure to preheat it to 350°F in your kitchen oven for at least one hour before starting to weld. Try to block the part to be welded up off the steel of your welding table so that the mass of the welding table will not pull the heat out of your weld assembly.

5. During and after welding, you may wire brush the weld area with a small stainless steel wire brush to clean the weld. Do not clean the weld or the seam with a brush that has copper, brass, or aluminum bristles, because the noncompatible bristles will transfer metal to the weld and eventually will cause the weld to crack.

Additional Tips for Cleaning Parts Prior to Welding

1. Liquid cleaning of the parts just prior to welding should also include acid cleaning if the parts are aluminum or lightly rusted steel. Acid cleaners are available from several sources, but paint stores are the easi-est place to find these liquid metal cleaners. Ask for a phosphoric acid solution. You may find it by trade names such as "OSPO," "Metal Prep," or by the chemical name, phosphoric acid. The costs for these metal cleaners will vary from $1.50 for one quart of phosphoric acid to $12.50 for a quart of name-brand metal cleaner. In most cases, you will need to dilute the phosphoric acid with 4 to 10 parts of water for use in removing rust and aluminum oxide from your parts. You can also find phosphoric acid in swimming pool and spa supply stores because it is used in pools and spas to keep the water in the correct pH range.

2. To clean aluminum parts prior to welding, prepare a mixture of phosphoric acid and water, and soak the parts in it for 30 minutes. Then remove the parts from the acid and rinse them in soft water and allow them to air dry. Do not blow-dry the parts with compressed air because most air compres-sors put oil into the air stream.

3. To clean rusty steel parts prior to welding, it is easier to mix up a 3:1 mixture of phosphoric acid (three parts water to one part acid), put the mixture in a spray bottle, and spray the parts to dissolve the rust. After soaking for 30 minutes, rinse the parts in soft water. Remaining rust will now sand or scrape off like old, cheap dried paint. It can also be wire brushed off in most instances.

Is This All a Lot of Work?

It takes a lot longer to read about how to do proper weld prep than it does to do it. On your next project, try doing a better preparation job and see if your welds look a lot better than ever before. Once you do this, you will find it easier the next time.

Use Only Vacuum-Melted M.C. Grade Welding Rods

In Chapter 12, you will read about welding rod that is worthy of

This custom-made CNC plasma cutter is about ready to make a special fishmouth plasma cut on a stick of 1/2-inch diameter 4130 tubing. *RANS, Inc.*

This 4130 steel tubing is grouped by part number for use in airplane fuselage assemblies. *RANS, Inc*

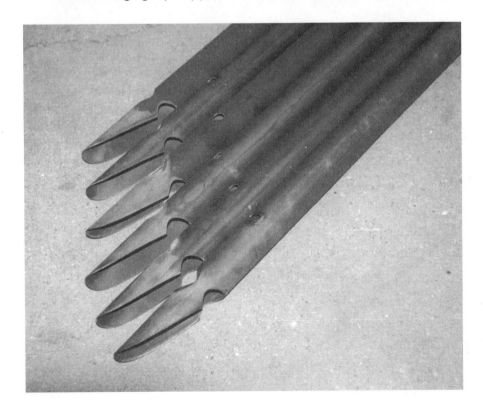

A close-up view of some intricate cuts made in 7/8 x .032-inch wall thickness tubing by the CNC plasma process. *RANS, Inc.*

the time you spend on your welding project, and the *best* rod only costs a little more than the paint that you will use to make your project look good. The best part is how much better your welds will be when you use the M.C. grade of welding rod.

Alternate Fitting Method

If you plan to notch a lot of small-diameter tubing, say 3/8-inch diameter, 1/2-inch diameter, and 5/8-inch diameter, it would be more economical to adapt milling machine end mills to your hole saw joint fitting fixture. When lubricated with cutting oil, an end mill will last for several hundred cuts, and it can be sharpened when it becomes dull.

A milling end mill cutter takes a few seconds longer to produce a fishmouth fit on a given size tube than a hole saw cutter does because the hole saw cutter only has to cut a thin line through the tubing, whereas the end mill has to eat away a full circle of metal to get through a given size tube.

Adapting an end mill to your joint fitting fixture works better than using hole saws because hole saws tend to shatter off all their teeth when cutting thin-wall, small-diameter tubing. This does not happen when using an end mill cutter.

Plasma Cutting

There are many advantages to plasma cutting, especially when you compare cutting chores to hand hacksaw cutting, oxyacetylene torch cutting, and the high cost of making dies for stamping out small parts.

The big advantage to plasma cutting is that it cuts all metals with equal ease. Plasma will cut 3/16-inch and 1/4-inch stainless steel plate into exhaust pipe flanges just as easily as it will cut the same thickness mild steel plate. And without changing settings, you can immediately cut out 6061-T6 aluminum plate for welding up special intake manifolds.

Stainless steel is one of the hardest of all the common shop metals to cut. It is so resistant to cutting that it will dull an expensive, high-speed bi-metal hacksaw blade in just a few seconds.

Cutting stainless steel plate or sheet, aluminum plate or sheet, 4130 steel plate or sheet, and brass and copper with plasma is almost as easy as drawing a line on the metal with a marking pen. But free-hand plasma cutting leaves an often shakey cut line, so you should try to provide a guide for your cuts with a plasma cutter.

And a finished product of RANS, Inc. is this S-7 Courier airplane. *RANS, Inc.*

A hole saw mounted in a drill press makes fast, accurate work of punching large holes in sheet steel.

Numeric Plasma Cutters

If you consider yourself to be in production, welding most of the day, every day, you should consider fitting your parts with a computer program-controlled plasma cutting setup. For many years it was possible to flame cut shapes and flanges by having an optically guided pantograph torch or a gang of torches follow a line drawing on a piece of white paper. That was a major step forward in mass production, but recent developments make it possible to produce even better and faster cuts in all metals with numerically controlled automatic plasma cutting machines. Talk to your welding equipment dealer about your special circumstances if you have the need to increase your production and the quality of your parts.

This chapter contains photos of an operation in Hays, Kansas, that makes excellent use of CNC plasma cutting to produce net-size cuts in 4130 steel tubing. The company is called RANS, Inc., and it builds large numbers of kit airplanes for the experimental aircraft market.

Band Saw Cutting

Any band saw that has a separate belt-driven drive wheel can be converted to cut steel and aluminum. The only band saws that cannot be easily converted are the "model makers" direct-drive saws.

If your band saw has a belt drive, you can substitute a compact speed reduction unit that provides you with at least three or four different output speed ratios. This can be done by adding two extra jack shafts to the base that the electric motor mounts on. Then you add extra belts and chains.

The first ratio from the motor to the first jack shaft should be V-belt drive, probably a 2:1 reduction with a 2-inch pulley on the motor and a 4-inch pulley on the jack shaft. Read Chapter 14, Shop Math, to figure out how to calculate compound gear or chain ratios. V-belts can slip when under lots of torque, so you will probably want to use a #35 pitch chain on the final low-speed ratio.

Blade Speeds

Because different brands of band saws have different diameters (and circumferences) of saw blade drive wheels, you have to calculate (using shop math) the correct rpm to turn your band saw to obtain the correct blade speeds. Blade speeds are always expressed in fpm (feet of blade travel per minute). I'll give you a common example of blade speed calculation on a specific band saw, then you can calculate the desired rpm numbers for your own band saw.

Let's say that your present band saw has an electric 1/3-horsepower motor that turns 1,725 rpm and your band saw drive wheel is 10 inches in diameter (31.416 inches in circumference). Every time the drive wheel turns one revolution, the blade is traveling about 31 1/2 inches, or slightly less than 3 feet per revolution. If your belt drive is a 2:1 unit, the band saw drive wheel is turning 863 rpm and the blade is traveling 27,096 inches in one minute. Divide inches by 12 to obtain 2,258 fpm of blade travel, which is great for sawing thin plywood but way too fast to saw aluminum or steel.

You need to slow the blade down with another 2:1 reduction ratio to saw aluminum at 1,126 fpm, or another 3:1 ratio to saw steel at 375 fpm. You can calculate the reduction ratios you need to set up for your particular band saw. The following charts give blade speeds for cutting metal.

Bi-Metal Blades

Always buy bi-metal band saw blades. The single-metal blades wear out much faster and never cut as well as bi-metal ones.

Cleaning Off Rust

It is acceptable to use 4130 steel tubing that has a thin film of rust on it if the rust has not pitted the metal noticeably. In fact, most tubular frames will start to rust just an hour or two after they have been tack-welded.

I have seen tack-welded airplane fuselages and race car frames hauled cross-country after they were tack-welded and before they were finished being welded and painted. When you haul bare steel down the highway in the rain and fog, you can expect rust to form on it.

The obvious thing you should do before taking a tack-welded or otherwise unpainted tubular structure out in the weather is to coat it with a spray preservative that can be wiped off easily with solvent at a later time. Spray lubricants such as WD-40 or LPS work well for temporary rust protection.

But if your tack-welded steel framework has already rusted slightly, the first thing to do is to wipe down the rust spots with a liquid metal prep that is ordinarily used in auto body shops for the same purpose. One brand that is easy to find in automotive parts stores that cater to body shops is PPG Metal Cleaner. It contains phosphoric acid, so use rubber gloves to apply it and apply it with a small piece of cloth or a small sponge. When it dries to a white film, wipe the film off with a Scotchbrite™ pad and you will see that the rust is gone. When the rust layer is significant, it may take two or three applications to clean off all the rust. Next time, you won't let your really good parts get rusty.

Reasons to Fit Parts Closely

Assuming you were taught to weld thick parts for trailers and structural steel, you were probably taught to V-grove thicker pieces of metal so the weld would penetrate all the way through the base metal. That method is correct, but only for thick (over .090-inch wall thickness) metal. When you are welding metal as thin as .005 inch to .049 inch, you should not have any space between the two or more parts.

The reason for tight fits on thin parts is that any air gap on the back side of the weld will allow for atmospheric contamination of the weld.

The front of the weld is protected from the atmosphere by the CO_2 when MIG welding, by the argon when TIG welding, and by the combined oxyacetylene flame when gas welding. But nothing protects the back side of the weld if you have big, wide gaps. You can expect crystallized back sides of the weld if you try to bridge wide gaps.

When welding a tube cluster of 3/4 x 0.32-inch tubing, a good tight fit protects the back side of the weld and prevents air from getting to it and contaminating it. Aluminum is less susceptible to contamination on the back side than steel, but even aluminum welds usually look very lumpy if the fit-up of the parts was bad or gaps were too wide.

Another reason to try for good, tight fit-ups on thin metal is that the weld bead will be much easier to control and therefore much easier to make perfect.

Bandsaw Blade Speeds Chart

Material	Matl. Number	Name	Feet-Per-Minute
Aluminum	6061	Weldable	1,200
Carbon Steel	1020	Mild Steel	330
Low Carbon Steel	4130	Chromemoly	270
Stainless Steel	308	Weldable	Not rec.
Inconel	600	Weldable	70
Titanium	99 percent	Pure	70
Titanium	Ti6A14V	Weldable	45
Bronzes	Most Grades		180
Plywood	to 1/2-inch		2,400
Oak	to 4 inches		1,800

Chart information from American Saw and Manufacturing Company.
Blade speeds must be accurate to avoid burning the blade.

Bandsaw Blade Teeth-Per-Inch Chart

Material	Thickness	Blade Teeth/Inch
4130 Steel	0.20 to .100-inch	14
1020 Steel	0.50 to .125-inch	10
4130 Steel	.100 to 1.000-inch	10
6061 Alum.	.050 to .125-inch	10
6061 Alum.	.125 to 6.000-inch	9
3-Ply Plywood	.063 to .250-inch	10
Solid Oak	1.000 to 4.000-inch	10
White Pine	.500 to 4.000-inch	6

Consult this chart for proper blade teeth. Half-inch wide blades are stronger than quarter-inch wide blades.

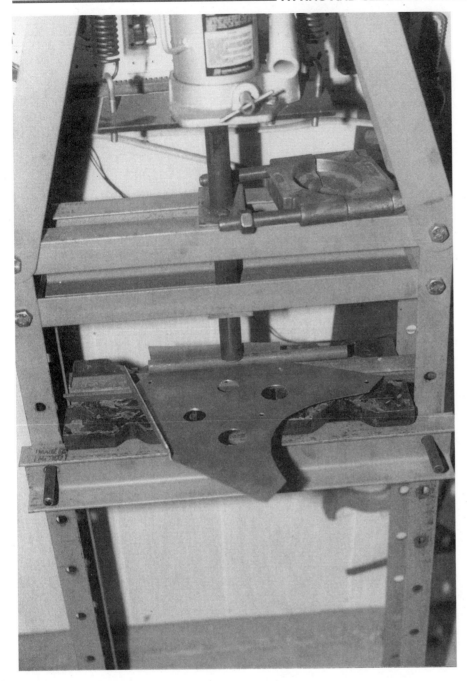

Smooth bends can be pressed into rather thick steel parts by using a hydraulic press, an angle frame, and a round steel bar.

CHAPTER FOUR

JIGGING

In the manufacturing and production business, the jigs that the parts are welded in usually are much heavier and more complex than the actual parts they hold. When you are producing several of a specific framework or assembly, a strong, intricate welding jig is actually a time- and materials-saving item.

But if you are only making one or two of a welded assembly, you can usually get by with a temporary, lightweight jig. Many times, a pair of vise grip pliers will do, and for sure, a batch of C-clamps is often the best way to clamp together something for welding. In this chapter, I will show you several ways to "jig" together parts for welding. Then you can be the judge of which of the pictured jigs will suit your project the best.

Permanent Welding Jigs

There is no magic number of welded assemblies that dictate when it is economical and useful to build a permanent welding jig. The answer is usually related to total time spent on fitting and welding and then, of course, accuracy and interchangeability.

If you were building free-form metal sculpture for wall decorations, you probably would not need a welding jig. But if you are building aircraft landing gear legs to be stocked as spares, you absolutely would want the landing gears to be a bolt-in fit every time. In that case, a simple but accurate welding jig would be a wise idea. Take a look at the Osprey II airplane landing gear welding jig in this chapter for one suggestion on building a simple but permanent welding jig.

In other situations, where speed and efficiency equals profit, steel framework welding jigs are a necessity. The two RANS, Inc., airplane-part jigs shown in this chapter make it relatively simple to weld up a complete fuselage in the jig, with assurance that the next 10 and the following 100 welded assemblies will all be identical and that the associated parts will

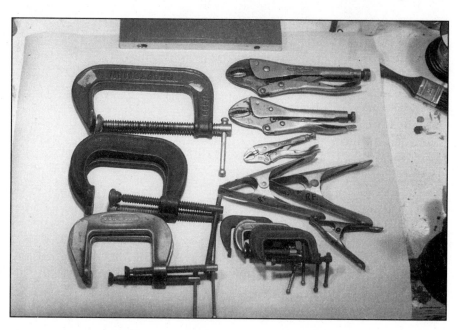

Several old standby methods of jigging your one-time welding projects are the C-clamps, vise grip clamps, and metal clothes pin-type clamps.

Simple 90-degree and 45-degree magnetic clamps will make your welding project easier to do. Buy several of these magnetic clamps.

William's Lo-Buck Tools makes this adjustable alignment tool that works great for many tubing and even-angle stock fit-ups.

bolt together without the need to file or drill anything.

Heavyweight welding jigs are not always the best solutions. It is a fact that a 2-foot-by-4-foot-by-1/2-inch solid steel plate can flex several thousandths of an inch with very little pressure. That means that welding up a tubular assembly that is simply bolted to the solid steel plate could still be able to twist or bend the plate as the tube structure is welded. If you are trying to maintain a few thousandths-of-an-inch of fit-up tolerance, the solid steel plate would not be rigid enough.

The best steel-welding jigs are ones that are light enough to be disassembled easily, and that are triangulated properly to prevent movement of the rig while the welding process is taking place. Bolt-together and pin-together welding jigs work well in most cases.

A perfect example of a very high-production automobile that was jig-welded was the production run of the Pontiac Fiero sports car. To ensure perfect body panel alignment, the body mount pads on the Fiero frame were all thicker than necessary at weld-up time so that when the space-frame chassis cooled after welding, automatic milling machines trimmed all the body mount pads to the perfect height. In this particular auto-building technology, the fit of the plastic body panels was considered to be of major importance.

Designing a Welding Jig

Often it is easier to build the first part to the dimensions on the plans and then make a jig to fit the first actual part. This is the design method used by many engineers who design welding jigs.

Another way to design a welding jig is to first cut out all the necessary parts from metal, fit them together, and then build a jig that will hold all the parts in place while they are welded. If the welded assembly is not too complicated, this method works pretty well.

Still another way to make a welding jig to fit a large structure, such as an airplane fuselage, is to design the welding jig from the blueprint that defines the fuselage. In one such case, I designed a rotatable welding jig for one of my airplane projects that defined the size and shape of the fuselage structure and at the same time it provided a weld fixture for a fuselage that measured 16 feet long, 4 feet wide, and 4 feet high.

That particular welding jig began with a 2 1/2-inch-diameter, .080-inch wall tube, 20 feet long. At specific inch station locations along the length of the 2 1/2-inch tube, fuselage bulkhead brackets were located. Then the bulkheads were attached to the brackets and the longeron tubes fitted to the bulkhead and tack-welded in place.

My friend, Dr. Phil Royal, built an aluminum plate and bolted an aluminum angle-welding jig so that he could build several identical landing gear legs for his Osprey II seaplane.

As the fuselage assembly progressed, the 2 1/2-inch tube provided a center point that allowed the fuselage structure to be rotated for ease of welding. As you likely know at this point, the easiest and best welds are the ones that can be made flat, not uphill, not overhead and not upside down. And, of course, the 2 1/2-inch tube rotated in sawhorse-type frames at each end.

Take a close look at the numerous welding jigs in this chapter and elsewhere in this book for ideas about how to design a welding jig for your project. There is no single, perfect way to design a welding jig, and the

second and third jigs you design will probably be better than your first one.

Weld Table Jigs

You have likely noticed the really artsy, polished stainless steel boat railings on pleasure yachts and even some ski boats. One particular shop in Santa Barbara, California, designs boat railings for each individual boat, and then they fabricate the railings on a 4-foot-by-8-foot welding table made of 3/8-inch steel plate.

It is easy to make a layout on the welding table top with a black magic marker pen. After the layout and the job are finished, the magic marker

lines and notes on the welding table top can be removed with acetone.

Since every boat railing is different, it would be too time-consuming and expensive to build a welding jig for each railing. Instead, the stainless steel railing base plates are tack-welded to the table top and the polished tubing (usually 1-inch O.D. x .065-inch wall) is then formed, trimmed, and welded to each base plate.

After the railings are completely welded, the base plate tack welds are cut off the steel welding table top with an abrasive cut-off wheel, the tack-welded spot is ground and polished smooth, and the new railing is taken

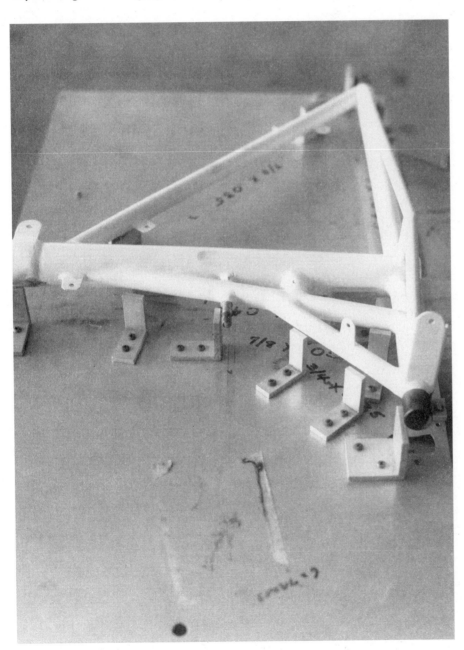

After the Osprey II landing gear leg was welded in the jig, it was sandblasted and powdercoated to prevent rust when landing in the water.

This particle board and white pine welding jig ensures proper alignment when welding up the sides on an experimental airplane.

An excellent fit-up of 4130 steel tubing members. TIG or MIG welding can be done on this particle board weld jig by clamping the ground to one of the tubes.

out to the yacht harbor and bolted to the deck of the pleasure yacht.

The tack welds on the welding table top are then ground away with a 4-inch hand grinder equipped with a #80 grit flap wheel. Next, the table is wiped down with acetone and made ready for the next boat railing job. The temporary welding jig served its purpose and can be changed to fit any size and shape boat deck.

Plywood Jigs

For many years, probably since the first steel tube fuselage airplane was built, welders have been building the fuselage structures on a plywood table top, much like how a stick-and-paper balsa flying model is built. Except that the framework on the model is glued rather than welded.

Take a look at the photos in this chapter and also the photos in Chapter 9, Gas Welding, to see how an airplane welding table is built. You will have to adjust the length and width of your plywood or particle board welding table to suit your project, but the basic design will be the same.

Just make sure that the height of the table is right so that you will have an easy stand-up welding layout. Kitchen cabinet work tops are designed for stand-up food preparation, so measure your kitchen cabinet top height and make your plywood or particle board table the same height.

After the table is built, you will need to make sure it is level to ease measuring and setting up the tubular structure. Small, tapered wood shims can be used to level the base of the table to the floor. A hot glue gun or epoxy glue will hold the tapered shims in place on the floor.

After one side of the airplane fuselage was tack-welded with a gas welding torch, the frame was removed from the jig so the second side could be built on the jig. See Chapter 9 for pictures of the completed fuselage.

A typical aircraft weld repair shop is this one at Wag Aero Group at Lyons, Wisconsin. *Wag Aero Group*

A tack-welded 4130 steel tubing airplane fuselage has been removed from its alignment jig for shipment to a customer, who will complete the welding on the tack welds, thereby saving several thousands of dollars in welding labor. *Wag Aero Group*

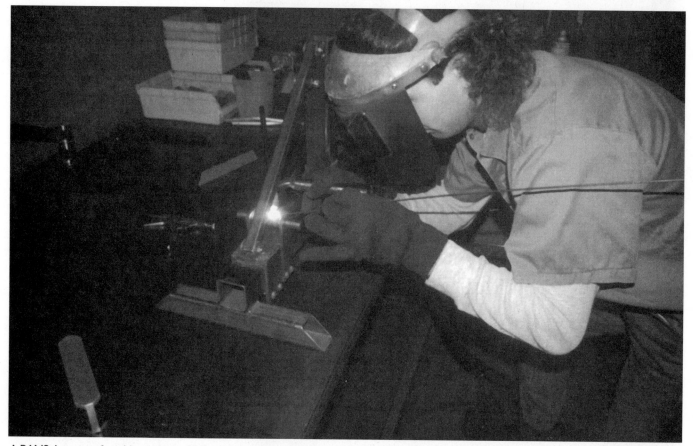

A RANS, Inc. aircraft welder is shown TIG welding a subassembly on a square tube welding jig that assures identical parts every time. *RANS, Inc.*

Even if you plan to TIG or MIG weld your fuselage structure, the plywood or particle board top will work well. To make electrical contact with your framework, simply clip the welding machine ground clamp to one of the main longerons or other part that will carry the welding current.

Don't spend too much time and money on plywood or particle board welding tables unless you plan to build several airplane fuselages to the same set of plans. And if that's the case, then you might take a little extra time to make the table more user-friendly.

Crude Weld Tables

Take a look at the simple plywood welding table in Chapter 9 that is merely a piece of 1/2-inch plywood resting on a bunch of rubber traffic cones! The traffic cones belonged to the SCCA sports car club, and I needed a quick layout table for a new sports car frame that I was building. Later, I finished the frame by placing the 4-foot-by-8-foot plywood sheet on a couple of carpenter's sawhorses. The end result was a class D sports race car that won numerous national class races and at least three race driver's championships. For a one-of-a-kind race car frame, a crude but effective plywood welding table proved to be completely adequate. A similar welding table might fit your needs, too.

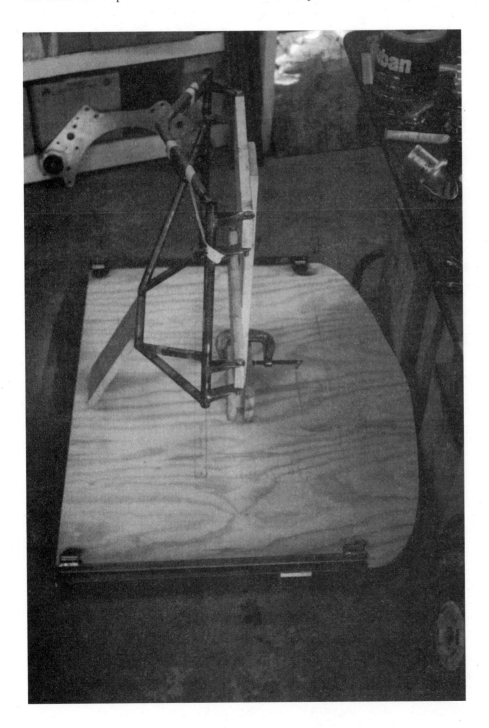

This engine mount welding jig was designed around the shape and actual size of the airplane firewall. Steel brackets locate the actual firewall mounting points.

A completed and painted airplane fuselage frame built in the welding jig shown above. *RANS, Inc.*

This light, rigid, and strong welding jig ensures that every airplane fuselage built in this jig will be identical to the others. The jig is made from thin-wall square tubing. *RANS, Inc.*

In order to ensure that dozens of Chevrolet V-6 engine mounts will fit on RV-6A kit airplanes, Jess Meyers of Belted Air Power, Las Vegas, Nevada, builds each mount in this simple but strong angle-iron welding jig. *BAP*.

CHAPTER FIVE

TIG WELDING 4130 STEEL TUBING

Like the proverbial foot journey that begins with one step at a time, TIG welding 4130 steel tubing begins with starting the arc, making a very small molten puddle, adding one dip of welding rod to the puddle, then pulling the rod out of the heat of the arc. If you do this arc welding process four or five times, you have made a tack weld. If you have done this welding process 15 or 20 times, you have welded halfway around a tubular joint. Repeating the process thousands of times means that your "journey" is complete: You have assembled a tubular frame by TIG welding it.

Preheating?

Here is another old wives' (old welders'?) tale that keeps being passed on by word of mouth: Chrome moly assemblies must be preheated by subjecting them to the flame of an oxyacetylene gas torch just before you begin welding them. This is incorrect, and doing so is just one more way to "hurt" your 4130 steel (chrome moly) structure. First of all, the experts say that preheating is not necessary for 4130 steel under 1/4-inch thickness. Then, the next reason to not torch-heat 4130 steel is that you really do not know what temperature it is heated to if you are just passing a flame over it. It could be anywhere between 100 degrees F to 1,000 degrees F, which is no way to preheat for welding. A third reason for not preheating your tubular 4130 steel structure is that it would be cooled back to ambient room temperature before you could complete the first 20 percent of the welds. So you gain nothing by trying to preheat a tubular

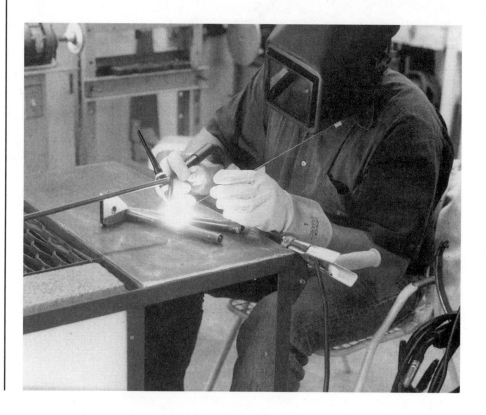

I am TIG welding two 4130 steel tubes together for a turbocharger bracket. I am using new, clean, lightweight gloves made specifically for heliarc welding.

This is the back side of a 300-horsepower, twin-turbocharged Aerostar engine. You can see the TIG-welded 4130 steel engine mount that was *not* stress-relieved after it was welded. Not a single one of over 1,600 identical engine mounts was stress-relieved, and not one ever cracked in use. Also note the intricately welded stainless steel exhaust system.

structure before welding, and you take the chance of harming it by application of an open-air flame.

It is certainly not a wise idea to weld a 4130 steel structure in a freezing workshop in the wintertime. The welding workshop should be shirt-sleeve comfortable, with a room temperature of 75 degrees F to 95 degrees F, even in winter. If it isn't, put a heater in the workshop. Welding cold metal *is* hard on the metal. But normal room temperature is acceptable for welding thin-wall tubing.

Fitting and Cleaning

Read Chapter 3 again and pay special attention to what it says about fitting the parts tightly. A "watertight" or a "daylight tight" fit is a lot easier to weld than a loose fit where you can see a big gap between the parts. Make sure you have cleaned the area that will be affected by the heat of the weld, and be sure to clean the welding rod. Most things that you will TIG weld will be capable of life support. In other words, the engine mount for an airplane will be a very critical piece of structure when it is put into use: holding the engine in an airplane. The front suspension of a race car will be equally as important when the race car is traveling at 200 miles per hour!

TIG Welding Procedure

Let's say that you are welding a tubing cluster of 7/8-inch O.D. x .049-inch wall 4130-N steel. Here is a good setup:
- Water-cooled torch, WP-10 size
- Number 8 ceramic cup
- 1/16-inch diameter 2 percent thoriated tungsten
- Argon gas, set to 20 CFH
- Pre-flow timer set to .5 second.
- Post-flow timer set to 10 seconds
- Amps set to 75, percentage set to 75 percent
- Polarity set to DC straight (DCSP)

- High frequency set to "start only."
- Tungsten ground to "pencil point" shape
- Tungsten stick-out 1/8-inch
- Foot pedal ready to operate to start the arc

The setup listed above is for the old "standby" welding machine. If you are fortunate and have one of the newer square-wave TIG welding machines, you have several extra options at your disposal. You will be

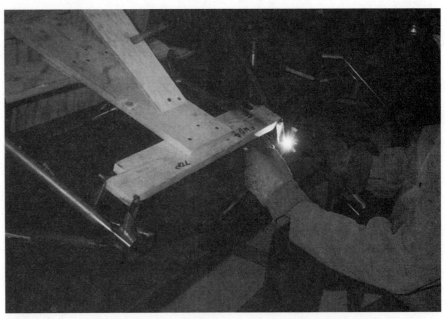

Dale Johnson is TIG welding a 4130 steel engine mount, jigged up in a wooden jig. The engine mount was not stress-relieved after it was welded, and it fit the airplane and Buick V-6 engine perfectly.

This is a typical Lycoming engine mount that was fabricated at the American Aircraft Factory in Cleveland, Ohio, in 1971. The mount was not stress-relieved after welding, and no cracks developed in over 1,600 hours of operation.

The white tubular frame in this picture is a TIG-welded 4130 steel engine mount used in a Helio Courier STOL airplane.

able to dial in a known "best setup," and you can also dial in a "crater fill" option. Or you can use the top-of-the-line welding machines just like you would an "old standby welding machine."

Torch Cup Sizes

The optimal ceramic cup size for most steel and stainless steel welding is a No. 8 because that size provides good argon flow for proper weld coverage, but it also allows you a good, unobstructed view of the weld puddle, too. When you are welding tubing, there will be tight corners that a No. 8 ceramic cup will not fit into. The thing to do in that situation is to temporarily go to a No. 6 cup or even a No. 4 cup, but be sure to go back to a No. 8 or No. 10 cup as soon as the access to the weld seam permits.

The problem with small cup sizes is that they do not distribute the 20 cfh argon flow as well as larger cups do, and you will have problems with air-contaminated welds, caused by using a cup that is too small.

Tungsten Stick-Out

Ideally, the tungsten should *always* be completely inside the argon gas flowing out of the cup. Yes, it is possible to extend the tungsten out of the cup by 1/2-inch or more, but it will often become contaminated (while the arc is active) by air, and then your weld instantly becomes contaminated.

This end view of an aircraft certification cluster shows at least 100-percent weld penetration and a flawless fit-up of the tubes to the plate.

These two welded tube clusters are both certified aircraft welding coupons that have passed certification inspection. If your welds can match these, you will probably be a good aircraft welder.

This tubular square frame was TIG-welded, then sawed through on the lower tube without stress-relieving. The very slight mismatch in the lower tube shows that almost no stresses were caused by TIG welding. In most situations, post-weld stress-relieving attempts can harm the structure far more than they will help it.

This white-painted engine mount made from formed 4130 steel sheet is another example of good TIG welding.

A close-up of the TIG welds on this four-cylinder LOM aircraft engine in an RV-4 kit plane lets you see the kind of welds to try for. Good workmanship is exhibited here.

The diameter of the welding rod, the diameter of the tungsten electrode, and the close fit-up of parts contributed to this very small and neat weld on a PT-6 engine mount.

The best procedure is to extend the tungsten past the cup by no more than one-half the width of the cup. If the cup is 1/2-inch across, let the tungsten stick out no more than 1/4-inch.

There will be corners to weld where a No. 4 cup is required to gain access, and you may need to let the tungsten stick out of the cup by up to 1/2-inch, but when you do that, you will be taking a big chance on contaminating the tungsten either by touching it with the welding rod or by touching the weld puddle with it. At all times try to make a No. 8 cup and a 1/16-inch tungsten work.

Stress Relieving After Arc Welding

Right up front, I will tell you that it is not possible to accurately stress relieve a welded 4130 steel assembly by heating it red-hot with an oxyacetylene torch in an open-air (or closed air) workshop.

Stress relieving a welded 4130 steel assembly such as an aircraft engine mount or a race car rear suspension

An Alaskan bush plane landing gear and brake caliper mounting plate shows the possibilities of unique engineering designs made possible by the use of TIG welding.

member is a metallurgical process that requires at least six hours to do correctly. The steel grain structure must be slowly brought up to about 1,150 degrees F, held at that temperature for several minutes to a couple of hours, then slowly cooled back to room temperature. This very specific process absolutely cannot be accomplished by a hand-held torch in a welding shop.

Aerostar Engine Mounts

At the Aerostar Aircraft Factory we built over 800 airplanes in eight years. Each twin-engine airplane had two engine mounts, of course, so we obviously built over 1,600 TIG-welded 4130 steel mounts. Not a single one of those 1,600 mounts was stress-relieved after welding. I recently called the FAA and the AOPA and asked for Aerostar maintenance and malfunction reports. Not one single

The Llama bush plane is built in Colorado and features a fully TIG-welded fuselage structure under the aluminum skin and white paint.

A close-up of the rear seat structure of the Alaska bush plane shows the lightweight and strong TIG-welded frame.

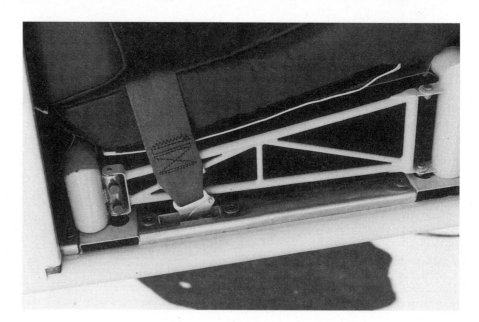

Aerostar engine mount has ever failed in service!

Even when a propeller blade came loose and caused the engine to tear out of the wing, the welds on the engine mount held. We did magnaflux-inspect every engine mount for cracks and porosity after welding, but none of the 1,600 engine mounts failed the magnaflux inspections.

The Aerostar engine mounts were made from 4130-N steel tubing, welded with DCSP (DC straight polarity) TIG welding, using high-quality certified 4130 steel welding rod (1/16-inch diameter, bare, not copper-coated). Special care was taken to ensure good fit-ups of the tubing, and all the mount tubes were cleaned with acetone before welding.

After welding, each mount was glass-bead cleaned and magnafluxed. Next, each mount was filled with an oil-based preservative called Braycoat, allowed to drain, and then the oil holes were plugged with pop rivets. The mounts were painted with green

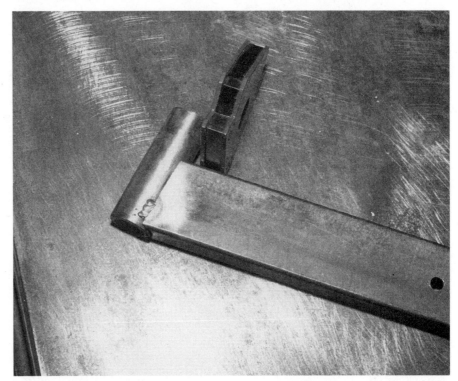

A TIG tack weld consists of about three drops (dabs) of 4130 welding rod to hold the tube to the rectangular member for fit-checking before complete welding.

Sheril Dickey's E-Racer airplane uses TIG-welded braces to align and retain its rear propeller bearing housing.

Emmerson Fittapaldi's Indy race car has a spindly but strong TIG-welded 4130 steel front suspension. It is chrome-plated and baked to normalize after the hydrogen embrittlement chrome plating is done.

Butler Racing, Inc., TIG welds its lower A-arm suspension on the Butler Cobra replica cars. After TIG welding, the A-arms are cadmium-plated to prevent rust.

Seth Hammond TIG welded this roll cage structure on his Bonneville record-holding race car because TIG welding is the most accurate and sound of all forms of manual welding.

Mooney Aircraft fabricates the nose landing gear assembly and the main landing gear assemblies by TIG welding 4130 steel tubing and 3/16-inch 4130 steel plate.

zinc chromate primer and then painted with silver epoxy paint. If you process your tubular 4130 steel-welded assemblies in the same way, you should have zero defects, too!

Tungsten Diameters

Two-percent thoriated tungsten, for welding steel and stainless steel, comes in sizes from a very tiny .020 inch up to a big 3/16-inch diameter. A good rule of thumb is to use a tungsten diameter that is about the same as the thickness of the steel part that you are welding. If you are welding .049-inch wall thickness 4130 steel, you would want a 1/16-inch (.063-inch) diameter tungsten electrode.

If you are welding .032-inch wall thickness tubing, use a .040-inch diameter tungsten. The chart below lists the diameter of tungsten, collets, and chucks you should have in your tungsten tray.

Tungsten Lengths

Standard lengths are 7 inches and 3 1/2 inches. It is less expensive to buy the 7-inch length and grind them in half for use with medium or short back caps. Using the full 7-inch-long tungsten with a long torch back cap is cumbersome, and the long back cap can get in your way. Avoid using the long back cap as much as possible.

Grinding Tungsten Points

There are two basic point shapes for all TIG welding, including aluminum welding. Use a pencil-point shape tungsten for steel and a crayon shape for aluminum.

The method you use to grind your tungsten points will directly affect the shape and control of your TIG arc. A crooked tip will give you a crooked arc. Often, the arc will even come off the side of the tungsten with a mis-shapen tip. Tungsten tips ground radially will encourage the arc to travel around in circles, following the circular grind marks on the tip.

The best tip on the tungsten is one that is a perfect cone shape with no grinding marks at all. One company, listed in Chapter 12, furnishes diamond ground tungsten, polished to 6 to 8 rms, compared to 75 rms for typical hand-ground tungsten.

Most good welding shops reserve a special #400-grit grinding wheel for

Inch-Decimal Wire Size Conversions

.020-inch	(0.5 mm)	diameter
.040-inch	(1.0 mm)	diameter
1/16-inch	(1.6 mm)	diameter
3/32-inch	(2.4 mm)	diameter
1/8-inch	(3.2 mm)	diameter
5/32-inch	(4.0 mm)	diameter
3/16-inch	(4.8 mm)	diameter

A welder from RANS, Inc., of Hays, Kansas, TIG welds a bracket to an airplane fuselage. *RANS, Inc.*

Dozens of airplane fuselage frames are completed at the RANS, Inc., airplane factory. *RANS, Inc.*

This stainless steel tubing "T" was purged with argon during welding and .020-inch 308 stainless rod was used to make a very tidy weld.

At least 50 separate pieces of #308 stainless steel were used to weld the lower inlet shape on this Turbo Tracker S-2 nose cowl. Just barely visible under the prop spinner area is a secondary heated inlet that was considered impossible to fabricate, but we did it!

George Morse TIG welded this clean and tidy stainless steel exhaust for his Rodek-Chevy-powered Jaguar sport airplane.

tungsten only. The reason you do not want to grind other metals on the same wheel that your tungsten is ground on is that steel from other grinding will adhere to the tungsten and contaminate it. Properly grinding your tungsten is just one of the many precautions you must observe in order to get high-quality welds.

TIG Torch Water Cables

If you are reasonably careful about dragging your torch cables over hot, just-welded places, you can weld for many months without ever scorching or melting holes in your TIG cables. I welded over 400 engine mounts in a two-year period before I accidentally (spell that "c-a-r-e-l-e-s-s-l-y") melted a small hole in

one of my TIG torch water lines.

The worst thing you can do with your cables is to cover them with a heavy leather shield that zips up or snaps shut. The weight and stiffness of leather or fabric cable shields will affect the accuracy and quality of your welds.

The lighter the weight of your TIG torch and its associated lines, the less fatigue you will experience while welding. Guiding a torch and cables that weigh just a few ounces is far, far easier than trying to guide a torch and leather-covered cables that weigh several pounds.

TIG Torch Sizes

For aircraft and race car welding, you should have a very compact

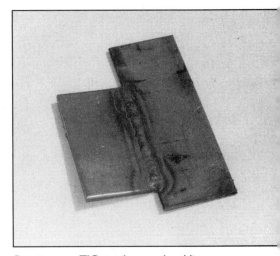

Practice your TIG stainless steel welding skills by butt-welding two pieces together like this, but argon purge the back side of the weld to prevent "sugar" in the weld.

Stage 2 Buick V-6 Indy Lights race cars, such as #38 shown here, make almost 100-percent use of TIG welding in chassis and suspension construction.

water-cooled torch that will accept the .375-inch diameter chucks and ceramic cups. The large, heavy-duty air-cooled and water-cooled torches are for nuclear powerplant welding and oil refinery pipe welding. This is another situation where one tool (your torch) should not be expected to do all jobs. You may decide to have two or even three different TIG torches in your welding tool cabinet.

The only reason for owning an air-cooled TIG torch is that you could do field repairs where water tanks or water-cooling radiators would not be easy to set up. In almost every case, a water-cooled torch works better than an air-cooled torch. (Chapter 2 tells about the best torches to buy.)

The almost-invisible weld seam on this blown small-block Chevrolet dragster exhaust is the result of: (1) a very good fit-up, (2) argon purge behind the weld, (3) .040-inch weld rod, and (4) a welder who took time to make his welds look good.

Pieces of straight and 180-degree curved stainless steel pipe were trimmed to fit and butt-welded to make the exhaust for this Buick V-6-powered GTP race car.

Vacuum Chamber TIG Welding

As already stated, stainless steel and titanium require protection for the back side of the weld bead to prevent *sugar*, or crystallization of the back of the weld bead. This is an easy thing to do when you are welding an exhaust manifold or a small oil or water tank where you can purge the back side of the weld simply by flowing 10 to 20 cubic feet of argon per hour to the weld area.

But when you are welding larger sheet metal assemblies such as the Grumman S-2 Turbo Tracker nose cowling shown in this chapter, a vacuum chamber is the only way to ensure sugar-free welds that will not crack after welding.

"Vacuum chamber welding" is something of a misnomer. The air (oxygen, hydrogen and other impurities) are evacuated from the weld chamber and the bad air is replaced with pure argon, making a completely inert atmosphere. Obviously, you would want to put several to-be-welded parts into the chamber so that you could weld them with only one evacuation and argon filling of the chamber, to conserve argon.

A good vacuum welding chamber can be made to operate at less than 1 part-per-million of O_2 (oxygen), H_2O (water) and N_2 (nitrogen), and less than 20 parts-per-million of H_2 (hydrogen). If your stainless or titanium welds require better back gas purging, consider using a vacuum chamber.

The rear wing framework on this blown Chevrolet dragster is TIG-welded 4130 steel, air foil shaped, and chrome plated after welding.

Butler Racing, Inc., of Goleta, California, TIG welded this beautiful chrome-plated mild steel exhaust system on one of its Cobra replica cars. No back side argon purging is required when welding mild steel tubing. *Butler Racing, Inc.*

Properties of Steel Versus Temperature

Temperature	Process or Condition	Color
2,900°F		
2,800°F		
2,700°F		
2,600°F	Liquid State	Melts
2,500°F		
2,400°F		
2,300°F		Dazzling White
2,200°F		
2,100°F	Forging-Hot Working	White
2,000°F		
1,900°F	Magnetism Is Lost	Bright Yellow
1,800°F	Carburizing	Lemon
1,700°F	Annealing	Orange
1,600°F	Normalizing	Salmon
1,500°F	Atomic Changes	Bright Red &
1,400°F		Scaling
1,300°F		Cherry Red
1,200°F	Atomic Changes	Blood
1,100°F	Stress Relieving	Red
1,000°F	Nitriding	Faint Red
900°F		
800°F		
700°F		
600°F		
500°F		
400°F		Black
300°F	Preheating For Welding	
200°F		
100°F		
0°F		

Information courtesy of Air Liquide America, Inc.

Huffaker Engineering built this successful Pontiac Fiero GTU race car by TIG welding many short pieces of 4130 steel tubing into a subframe for the fiberglass body.

Tim Marr of Lincoln Electric Company demonstrates a thumb-button-operated TIG torch on a couple of stainless steel plates. No foot control is needed with this arrangement.

Every part of the front suspension on this dragster right front wheel is TIG welded for maximum strength. Because it is a one-of-a-kind suspension, vacuum oven stress relief was done after welding.

Another one-of-a-kind Camaro race car chassis features mostly TIG welding for accuracy and ultimate strength.

Stress Relieving After Welding

One of the most repeated and most taught mistakes in aircraft welding is that each welded assembly must be stress relieved after welding by reheating the welded area to blood red by heating it with an oxyacetylene torch, a process that usually takes less than two minutes to complete.

The fact is that this quick reheating process actually does far more damage to the welded tubular structure than it ever does good. The metallurgically correct procedure for stress relieving a welded assembly such as an aircraft engine mount is described below:

1. First, a suitable, heavy, corrosion-proof fixture must be built to support the welded engine mount while it is oven-heated to blood red, so the mount will not twist and warp.

2. Next, the mount and its supporting fixture must be put into a

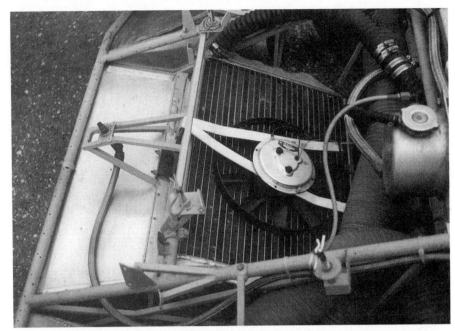

Thin-wall tubing, much like the tubing used in airplane fuselage structures, supports the radiator and front body panel on this Chevy Camaro road race car.

A Wag Aero TIG welder makes a repair on a stainless steel aircraft muffler. He should be wearing gloves to protect his hands from the radiation caused by the UV rays during TIG welding. *Wag Aero Group*

vacuum oven for a four- to six-hour heating and cooling process.

3. The temperature of the oven is slowly brought up to about 1,250 degrees F, taking about four hours to heat the mount from room temperature to the temperature where the metallic grain structure changes to fully relieve stresses. The temperature is held at this number for several minutes to an hour to ensure total relaxation of the metal grain structure.

4. Next, the heat is removed from the oven and the engine mount structure is allowed to cool naturally in a still-air condition, preferably in the vacuum of the oven.

5. Any attempt to speed up this process will result in possible hardening of the structure, crystallization of the weld area, and the formation of cracks in the heated area.

Scaling

Another noteworthy side-effect of torch heating welded tubular or plate structure another time after the initial weld has been completed is the obvious scaling and flaking of the surface of the 4130 steel. What this means in terms of strength is that a thin layer of the metal has been removed by the second heating process. This means that your .032-inch wall thickness tubing is now only .029 inch or even less because you caused a thin layer of the tubing to evaporate when you heated it again.

Temperature Control

In order to correctly relieve stress on a welded 4130 steel thin-wall tubing assembly, a very narrow temperature range must be reached and held for several minutes. This temperature is usually 1,125 degrees F to 1,265 degrees F, a range that is virtually impossible to attain with a hand-held oxyacetylene torch.

To quote the chart that has been provided by Tempil Division of Air Liquide American Corporation: *Stress relieving* consists of heating to a point below the lower Transformation Temperature, then holding for a sufficiently long period to relieve locked-up stresses, then slowly cooling." Stress relieving is a very accurate process.

We are looking through the observation port in a vacuum chamber used for TIG welding stainless steel and titanium parts without atmospheric contaminants. *Vacuum Atmospheres Company*

This vacuum chamber welding chamber makes it easy to get contamination-free welds on stainless steel and titanium parts. The chamber is actually filled with low-pressure argon gas after the atmosphere is pumped out of the tank. *Vacuum Atmospheres Company*

This multiport lexan sphere is custom-built to provide a pure argon atmosphere for welding stainless steel pipe. *Vacuum Atmospheres Company*

Pre- and Postpurge

There is a very good reason for the pre- and postpurge settings on a good TIG welding machine. The pre-purge of about one-half second is to ensure that argon gas will be covering the weld area when the arc starts. Otherwise there would be immediate contamination of the weld and the tungsten when the weld begins. If your welding machine does not have a pre-purge setting, hit the pedal and start the argon flowing for a second before you strike the arc.

After you finish the weld, do not immediately remove the torch from the weld. Hold the torch over the cooling weld for a count of 5 to 10 seconds to allow the argon postflow to cool and protect the weld until it cools below the critical contamination temperature. On clean steel and stainless steel, you can actually see the argon protecting the weld by not letting it change colors as it cools.

This aircraft factory welder is producing many of the same items every day. Notice that his TIG torch cables (wrapped around his neck for support) are not covered in heavy leather. But he is asking for radiation burns on his arms because he is welding aluminum with a short-sleeved shirt, a *no-no*.

CHAPTER SIX

TIG WELDING ALUMINUM AND MAGNESIUM

Once you get the hang of it, TIG welding aluminum becomes the easiest of all welding processes. You just have to observe some rules. The main difference in welding aluminum versus welding steel is that steel changes color as it heats up to the melting point for welding, but aluminum does not change color while heated to its melting point.

We'll have more on that later in this chapter. First, however, we should determine the kind of welding equipment you need to do aluminum TIG welding.

TIG Equipment for Aluminum

It makes almost no sense to have a TIG welder that will not weld aluminum. You must have a welding machine that has AC current plus high frequency, or a machine that has square-wave AC capabilities. You cannot weld aluminum and magnesium with a DC-only machine. The reason that AC current is required for welding aluminum is that aluminum and magnesium naturally contain oxides that cannot be cleaned off by DC welding. The sine wave characteristics of AC plus high frequency aids greatly in keeping the oxides from contaminating the weld puddle.

Read Chapter 2 to see the best TIG welder for aluminum. The right welder will make aluminum welding a very easy task.

Clean the Parts

One of the secrets to making really pretty welds in aluminum and magnesium is to clean and fit the parts properly. But if you use a sanding disc to clean the parts, you will

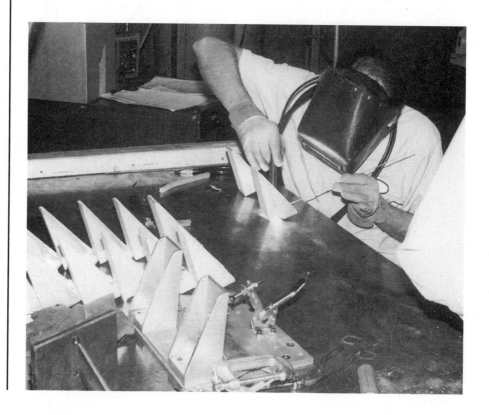

imbed small particles of sanding disc material into the surface to be welded. These small particles will contaminate your welds. And if you use a power wire brush to clean the parts, the steel bristles in the wire brush will erode off into the aluminum or magnesium and cause contamination in your welds. There are at least two solutions to the cleaning problem, however: caustic and plastic.

Caustic Cleaners

It is not easy to go to a chemical supply business and order phosphoric acid or other metal-etching chemicals simply by asking for a steel-cleaning chemical or an aluminum-cleaning chemical. You will probably have to buy a proprietary, brand-name cleaner that is sold to clean various

The big ceramic cup with the small opening on this TIG torch means that the torch is equipped with a gas lens collet for better welds on aluminum.

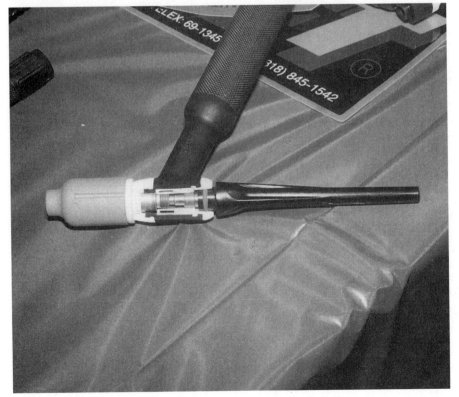

Another gas lens cup TIG torch that is cut away to show where the water passages are that cool the collet during welding. This is the best kind of torch to use for aluminum welding.

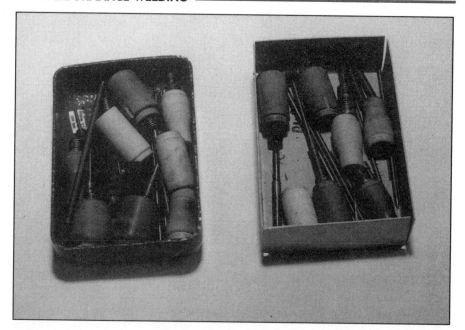

Here you see two separate trays that hold my TIG-welding parts. One tray is painted red and holds my 2 percent thoriated tungsten parts for welding steel. The other tray is painted green and holds all my pure tungsten for welding aluminum.

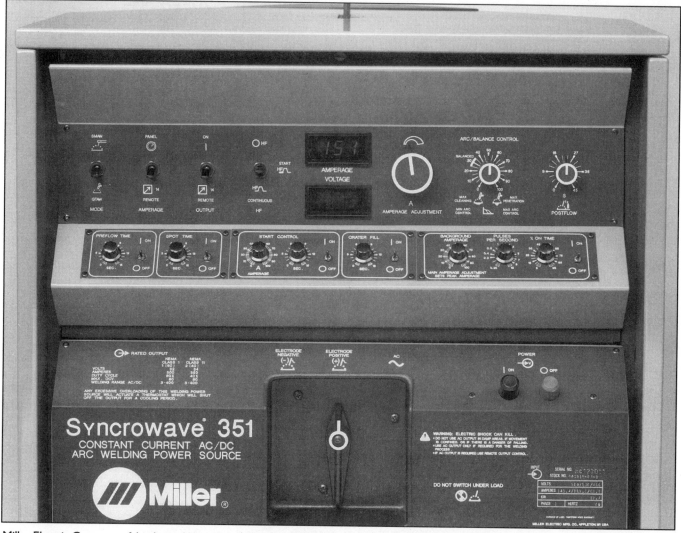

Miller Electric Company of Appleton, Wisconsin, makes this TIG welder, which can make the average welder look like a pro. This machine makes it possible to make the special adjustments that are described in the Arc Balance Control chart in this chapter. *Miller Electric Company*

metals. And, of course, you will have to pay a lot extra for the brand name on the plastic bottle.

Easy places to find metal cleaners are automotive body and paint supply stores and commercial paint stores. Ask for liquid cleaners, not paste. You want cleaners that will rinse off with water.

Plastic Cleaners

The best thing to use to clean aluminum for welding is a Scotchbrite type pad. The regular kitchen pot scouring pads work pretty well, and now 3M has a pad that clips on a circular wheel that can be operated by an air angle grinder motor or even a 1/4-inch drill motor. These plastic-based scouring pads work well to clean surface oxides off aluminum

and magnesium before welding. And, of course, just before welding, be sure to degrease the parts by wiping them down with acetone.

Aluminum Heat Transfer

Aluminum will soak up the torch heat a lot faster than steel, which means that you have to start off a little hotter (more amps) when you are TIG welding. In fact, it is even a good idea to use the next diameter larger tungsten electrode when you are TIG welding aluminum compared to the tungsten diameter you use for welding steel.

The result of a too-small-diameter tungsten is that under high heat, the tungsten will often splinter and sometimes it will even break off while you are welding. So start with a tungsten

one diameter larger than you would use if you were TIG-welding steel.

Because aluminum transfers heat more than other metals, expect the entire part to get hotter than the same part would if you were welding steel. It is not a problem, but it is good to know that this is a normal condition. Also be aware that aluminum will not change colors like steel as it is heated. First, it gets slightly more dull than when it is at room temperature, then it starts to get shiny, and then very quickly, a molten puddle forms where the heat is being applied.

Aluminum Arcing

Aluminum is notably less conductive electrically than steel is. This means that your aluminum part will tend to arc where it rests on the

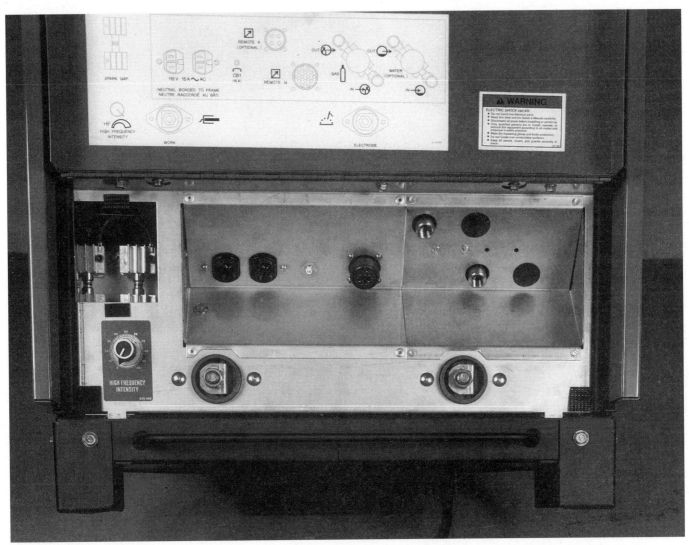

When you lift the hinged door on the front bottom of the Miller Synchrowave 351 machine, you will see the high-frequency spark gap copper contacts that must be cleaned and adjusted periodically, usually once a year. *Miller Electric Company*

Flat .050-inch thick 6061-T6 aluminum sheet was trimmed and formed into four separate pieces to make this round defroster duct adapter for my airplane.

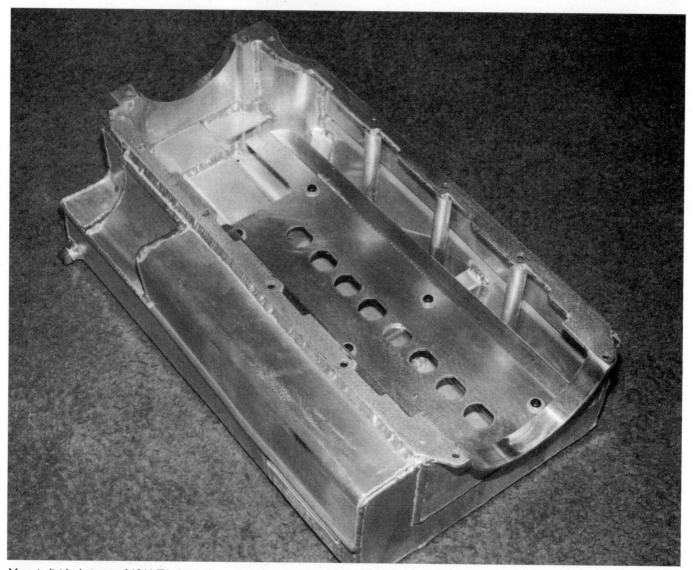

Many individual pieces of 6061-T6 aluminum were put together by TIG welding to make this race car oil pan. Billet Fabrication of Simi Valley, California, makes these lightweight pans.

grounded steel welding table. The result of this arcing at the weld table will be noticeable pitting and burning of the aluminum where it touches the weld table.

The best way to prevent this arcing and burning is to provide a positive ground for the aluminum part in addition to where it rests on the table, usually, a "welder's finger," a steel rod that rests on the welding table and on the part to be welded. The metal finger should have some weight to it to provide stability and to make a clamping-type electrical connection. I usually make several "welder's fingers" out of 3/8-inch steel rod and 1/2-inch diameter steel rod. Just don't let your aluminum parts arc on the welding table while you are welding.

Balling Tungsten

In welding school, the teacher taught all the students in my class to purposely ball the tip of the pure (not thoriated) tungsten before

Seth Hammond of Goleta, California, welded these lightweight aluminum valve covers for his record-holding Bonneville race car. It went 278 miles per hour in 1992. Another local company welded the sheet aluminum intake manifold.

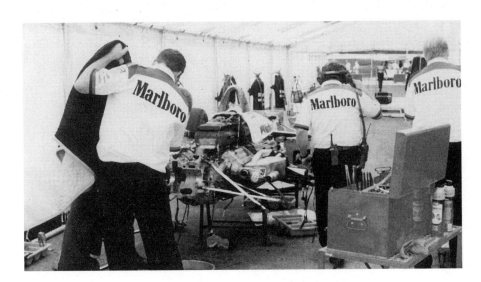

Roger Penske's Mercedes-powered Indy race car features a lot of TIG welding in the radiator cooling system. Here, the Penske mechanics hide their faces from my camera, and one prepares to throw a blanket over the rear axle area. Ah, racing!

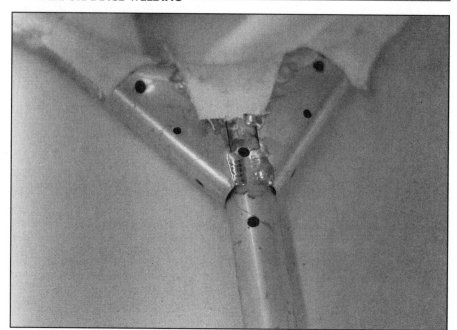

My airplane seat frame is made out of 6061-T6 aluminum and is TIG-welded. You see here that 100-percent welds are not always used, just enough weld bead to make the seat strong.

TIG aluminum welding is used to build the radiator and water lines for this Buick V-6 Indy Lights race car cooling system.

Griffin Radiator always does a beautiful job of welding aluminum radiators for all sizes of cars and airplanes.

I am getting ready to install the brackets for this Griffin aluminum radiator in Patrick Lockwood's 1964 Chevelle street/drag car.

making aluminum welds. For a while, I obediently balled the tungsten by first setting the welding machine to DC and positive polarity, striking an arc on scrap aluminum or copper, and holding the arc until the tungsten tip melted from a crayon-

Before you tackle a delicate TIG-welding job, practice on some scrap pieces of the same material.

shape into a round, shiny ball shape. The teacher told us that we must always follow this "tungsten balling" procedure in order to TIG-weld aluminum.

Then one day I didn't do the balling procedure and I just began TIG-welding aluminum using AC current with constant high frequency, and the tungsten worked just fine! I admit that in about 5 minutes of welding the pure tungsten did start to form a tiny little round ball right on the end of the crayon-shaped tip. But it was doing a better job of TIG welding aluminum than when I welded with the ritualistic big-balled tungsten! So I now always save myself a lot of trouble, and I no longer do the tungsten-balling ritual. I have found that a properly shaped and carefully sharpened tungsten will weld aluminum and magnesium just fine without going through this age-old balling process.

Welding Machine Settings

You should begin welding aluminum by practicing on several pieces of scrap before you tackle a job that will fly on an airplane or run on a race car. You should be able to run practice weld beads on small 2- x 2-inch pieces of thin aluminum sheet material. I like to practice on .020-inch to .050-inch thickness pieces of scrap aluminum. Next are the standard settings for most AC/DC TIG-welding machines:

• Polarity switch to AC
• High Frequency switch to Continuous
• Remote foot pedal switch to Remote
• Argon gas flowmeter to 20 cfh (cubic feet/hour)
• TIG-STICK switch to TIG
• Power switch to On

Note: if you have a square-wave machine, it may or may not have a high-frequency switch.

TIG welding a larger aluminum tube to the automotive air conditioner evaporator converted it into a light and efficient engine-cooling radiator for a stand-mounted Mazda aircraft engine. Read Chapter 11 on safety before TIG welding things that have had oil in them, such as this aluminum evaporator.

A converted Mazda rotary engine uses a well-built, intricate, aluminum oil pan. Preheating this assembly would make it easier to weld.

A nice TIG weld on Al Haralson's radiator expansion tank neck for his Mazda engine test stand. Try to make your TIG welds look this nice and smooth.

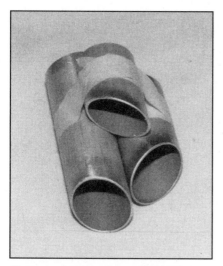

Cut several pieces of scrap 6061-T6 aluminum tubing into angles so you can practice making good welds before you tackle a serious project.

Striking the Arc

The easiest way for a TIG welding beginner to learn to start an arc for welding aluminum is to rest the torch ceramic cup edge on the aluminum surface with the tungsten resting about 1/4-inch from the aluminum. When you depress the foot pedal about halfway, the arc should start, similar to a spark plug arc starting.

Note: Do not touch the tungsten to the aluminum to start the arc!

Anytime you touch the tungsten to the aluminum or the aluminum welding rod to the tungsten while you are welding, you will get a big flash of light from the weld and you will get a lot of black soot on the weld. You will also get a sizable ball of aluminum on the tungsten. You can't continue to

weld when this happens. You also end up with a lot of soot on the part, and soot doesn't weld, so you'll need to clean it, too.

Stop and clean the ball of aluminum off the tungsten. A sanding belt is a good way to do this, or a #80 grit flap wheel, or a bench grinder will also clean the ball of aluminum off the tungsten. Otherwise, you would have to break the tungsten off at the aluminum ball, and that wastes a lot of expensive tungsten.

Why Does Aluminum Contaminate the Tungsten?

Remember that the temperature of the TIG arc is about 6,000 degrees F and that aluminum melts at about 1,150 degrees F. When the hotter tungsten touches the relatively cooler

The TIG-welded aluminum radiator and aluminum expansion tank save several pounds of weight in this ARS race car.

Another Buick V-6 Indy Lights race car has numerous tanks, pipes, and fittings that are TIG-welded aluminum. Race car and aircraft welders cannot get along without a TIG-welding machine that welds aluminum.

aluminum puddle, the cooler aluminum wants to flow to the hotter metal by capillary action. It "wicks" up on the tungsten and temporarily contaminates it. But if you continue to try to TIG weld with aluminum-contaminated tungsten, the 6,000 degrees F heat of the electrode will boil or burn off the aluminum in small amounts that will badly smoke up your weld. So don't try to weld with contaminated tungsten.

Aluminum Weld Procedure

Once you have learned to melt a puddle on a piece of aluminum, smoothly dip the end of your welding rod into the puddle, then pull the welding rod back about a 1/2 inch. Then continue to dip and pull the welding rod back, and you will see your beautiful weld bead progress. I dip about every 2 seconds. For practice, say, "dip, dip, dip, dip "

and develop a rhythm of dipping the rod into the puddle. A little practice will begin to pay off.

Square-Wave Welders

Welding technology for the 21st century includes square-wave technology. In the standard mode, AC welders incorporate a sine wave that is a series of positive and negative pulses of electricity, shaped like half circles, one above a zero current line and one below the zero current line. This cycle of positive and negative pulses occurs 60 times each second, 3,600 times per minute, and 216,000 times per hour.

But in square-wave welding, the positive and negative pulses stay at their peaks of plus and minus for much longer periods. Rather than the sine wave (rounded corners), the square wave has square corners. This square configuration allows the AC

TIG Welding Tips for Aluminum

• If in doubt about the alloy of the aluminum, use #4043 rod. The 4043 rod works in almost every situation.

• Use the diameter of rod that equals the thickness of metal; i.e., with .065-inch metal, use 1/16-inch rod.

• Use a gas lens cup for aluminum if possible. It makes prettier welds.

• Aluminum butt welding usually "keyholes" the seam. Just keep filling the keyhole with welding rod.

• Have at least three sizes of aluminum welding rod available for all sizes of beads.

• Use only high-quality certified welding rod.

• Don't attempt to weld aluminum after the tungsten has become contaminated.

• Use only pure tungsten for aluminum. Thoriated tungsten contaminates aluminum.

current to spend more time cleaning and more time heating the metal being welded, which is usually aluminum or magnesium.

Square-wave welding is not available in DCSP (DC current, straight polarity) when welding steel. It is only available in AC welding.

Square-Wave Variations

Study the chart in this chapter that illustrates the different settings possible with a full-featured square-wave welding machine. Four major, independently adjustable functions of the asymmetric power source are

• Frequency in cycles (Hertz) per second
• Electrode negative current level in amps
• Electrode positive current level in amps
• Balance (the percentage of time the electrode is negative)

Advantages of Square Wave

• More efficient control results in higher travel speeds
• Narrower, more deeply penetrating arc
• Ability to narrow or eliminate the etched zone
• Improved arc stability
• Reduction in use of high frequency

Low End Square-Wave Welders

The selling price difference in nonadjustable square-wave welders and the fully adjustable square-wave welders varies from $1,300 all the way up to $10,000. The low-end square-wave welding machines do a pretty

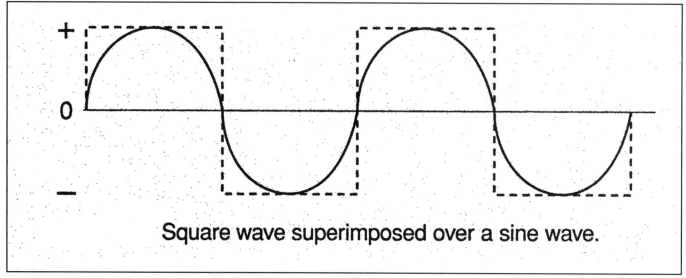

Square wave superimposed over a sine wave.

The solid curved line in this illustration indicates the shape of a normal AC sine wave used in TIG welding. Each peak and valley of the sine wave equals one cycle (Hertz). The dashed line shows how a square-wave AC welder reshapes the same AC cycle (Hertz) to provide longer cleaning time and longer heating time. *Miller Electric Company*

With an asymmetric AC TIG welder, the clean and weld times can be shaped to better suit the welding process. *Miller Electric Company*

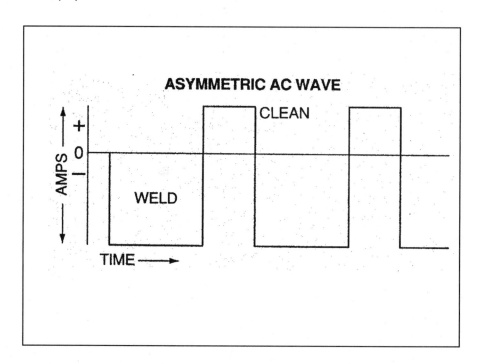

good job on aluminum sheet as thin as .010 inch. The top-of-the-line, fully adjustable asymmetric square-wave welding machines can adequately weld a crack in a big aluminum-block V-8 racing engine without preheating, and they can do a beautiful job on welding cracks in preheated aluminum cylinder heads. The choice of machine is determined by the money in your budget and the demands of the aluminum welding you expect to do.

High Frequency

High-frequency AC current is added to the AC or DC current to initiate a spark-jump arc so the tungsten does not have to touch the weld metal to start the arc. It is also added to (superimposed over) the pulsating current of AC welding to make the arc more stable and to keep the arc from going out at lower settings.

There has always been a lot said about the possible negative effects of high frequency on television sets and computers in the neighborhood when welding with AC high frequency. The suggestions is that high frequency can burn out your TV or your computer, and I suppose that this is a very good possibility. However, I have never heard of such an occurrence. I have welded aluminum with AC current and high frequency as close as 20 feet from several active computer systems, and I did not even make a blip on their screen. The key safety precaution is a good ground to carry off any stray high-frequency voltage before it reaches valuable electronic equipment such as computers.

TIG Welding Magnesium

Magnesium can catch fire and burn, and when it does, it's almost impossible to extinguish, so just stand back and let it burn. But magnesium does not usually catch fire unless there is magnesium powder or filings in the fire. So don't worry too much about welding magnesium castings.

Magnesium castings weld about like aluminum castings, except that magnesium seems to be more shiny while it is being TIG welded. During the TIG welding process, magnesium welds almost exactly like aluminum. However, be sure to use the correct magnesium welding rod. Read Chapter 12 to find out about magnesium welding rod.

TIG Welding Aluminum Heads

Typically, aluminum automotive cylinder heads and aluminum aircraft cylinders are very easy to weld when the need arises to repair cracks, ruined threads and loose valve seats and valve guides. Like any other aspect of welding, the basic rules apply:

• Clean the head or cylinder by completely removing all traces of carbon, preferably by chemical parts cleaning, then rinsing in clear, clean water.

Several wing ribs in this Aerostar right side wing were TIG welded to make sealed-off fuel bays in the wing. Even the Space Shuttle has a 6061-T6-welded crew compartment for pressure sealing while in orbit.

• Use a die grinder to vee out the crack or to remove pounded-out metal where the valve seat came loose. In some cases, bits of broken valve seats may still be imbedded in the combustion chamber, so be sure to grind them out.

•Vee-grind all cracks deep enough to assure 100 percent penetration of the crack when welding, or the unwelded part of the crack will propagate back into the weld.

Preheat

You can't easily clamp the head into or onto a steel welding fixture, so you should expect a slight amount of warpage from the welding and heat-treating process. Expect to resurface the head to remove warpage after welding.

Do not expect to preheat an aluminum head by using an oxyacetylene torch, because you just cannot control the heat of the torch accurately enough to do a proper job of preheating to 350 degrees F. An oven is the only accurate way to preheat a cylinder assembly or a cylinder head. To ensure a complete preheat, the head should be preheated at least one hour at 350 degrees F, immediately before beginning welding.

Welding Rod

Chapter 12 will tell you more about the proper rod to use, but I'll save you a little trouble now and tell you that 3/32-inch #4043 rod is a good choice to start with. You may also want to have several sticks of 1/16-inch and 5/64-inch rod on hand. Just remember that the diameter of the welding rod has a direct effect on the size of the completed weld bead.

Tungsten and Cup Size

You ought to start with a rather large torch cup, such as a No. 10, and at least a 3/32-inch diameter pure tungsten, and if that is not enough, use a No. 12 cup and a 1/8-inch pure tungsten.

And by all means, a water-cooled torch is the best way to weld thick aluminum castings. Air-cooled torches will get too hot and may affect the quality of your welds.

Check out Chapter 2 for information about which welding machines do the best jobs on repair welding large aluminum castings.

Weld Repair of Valve Seats, Aluminum Heads

One of the facts of life when using aluminum engine cylinder heads is that there are two kinds of aluminum cylinder heads: those heads that have had valve seat inserts come loose and those heads that *will* have valve seat inserts come loose if run long enough.

Heating and cooling cycles in cast aluminum tend to take out the temper (heat treat) and soften the aluminum. When the aluminum gets soft enough, and the valve has pounded the seat insert a few million times, the seat insert often comes loose and really hurts the cylinder, combustion chamber and piston.

But do not fear, loose valve seats in aluminum cylinders and cylinder heads are very easy to repair if you have the proper equipment. Proper equipment includes cleaning and degreasing equipment, preheating equipment, a TIG welding machine with at least 200 or more amps power (the new square-wave machines are the best), and a milling machine for refinishing the head after it is repair-welded.

Build-up Procedure

After the head is completely cleaned and preheated, the damaged seat area is welded in nice, smooth layers of weld bead to build up the aluminum high and thick enough so that there will be plenty of metal to support remachining the valve pocket out for a new valve seat insert.

The first time you try valve seat repair by TIG welding, practice on a scrap cylinder head until you get a good feel for how the bead should look. Actually it is even enjoyable to make TIG weld repairs on aluminum castings. It is a lot like applying clay to a clay pot to build it up. Proper preparation and welding rod filler material make the job quite easy.

Weld Fixture

If the aluminum part you are welding is something thin and light, such as a transmission tail shaft housing, expect it to shrink if you don't clamp it to a steel fixture to hold it in shape. The steel clamping fixture should be at least 3/8-inch thick, and the aluminum part should be bolted to it before you put it into the oven to preheat it.

You should leave the aluminum part bolted to the steel holding fixture while you weld it and until it cools. If you need to heat-treat the aluminum part after welding it, the steel holding fixture could be clamped to it to control shrinkage. The steel, however, needs to be rated to the aluminum. In other words, if you are welding an aluminum tail shaft housing that weighs 3 pounds, the steel holding plate you bolt it to should weigh at least 15 to 20 pounds. This means that the weight (mass) of the steel holding plate/fixture will be enough to control most of the aluminum casting tendency to shrink when it is heated by welding it.

CONTROLLING THE ASYMMETRIC POWER SOURCE

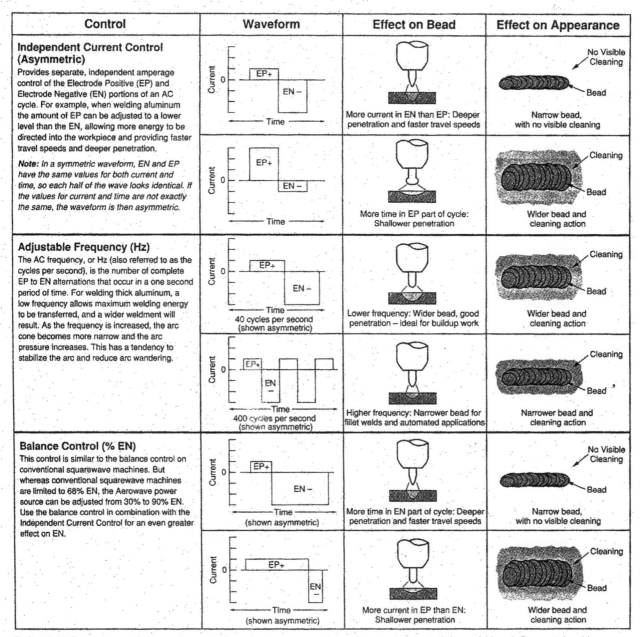

Control	Waveform	Effect on Bead	Effect on Appearance
Independent Current Control (Asymmetric) Provides separate, independent amperage control of the Electrode Positive (EP) and Electrode Negative (EN) portions of an AC cycle. For example, when welding aluminum the amount of EP can be adjusted to a lower level than the EN, allowing more energy to be directed into the workpiece and providing faster travel speeds and deeper penetration. *Note: In a symmetric waveform, EN and EP have the same values for both current and time, so each half of the wave looks identical. If the values for current and time are not exactly the same, the waveform is then asymmetric.*	*(waveform: EP+, EN−, Time)*	More current in EN than EP: Deeper penetration and faster travel speeds	No Visible Cleaning / Bead Narrow bead, with no visible cleaning
	(waveform: EP+, EN−, Time)	More time in EP part of cycle: Shallower penetration	Cleaning / Bead Wider bead and cleaning action
Adjustable Frequency (Hz) The AC frequency, or Hz (also referred to as the cycles per second), is the number of complete EP to EN alternations that occur in a one second period of time. For welding thick aluminum, a low frequency allows maximum welding energy to be transferred, and a wider weldment will result. As the frequency is increased, the arc cone becomes more narrow and the arc pressure increases. This has a tendency to stabilize the arc and reduce arc wandering.	*(waveform: EP+, EN−, Time)* 40 cycles per second (shown asymmetric)	Lower frequency: Wider bead, good penetration -- ideal for buildup work	Cleaning / Bead Wider bead and cleaning action
	(waveform: EP+, EN−, Time) 400 cycles per second (shown asymmetric)	Higher frequency: Narrower bead for fillet welds and automated applications	Cleaning / Bead Narrower bead and cleaning action
Balance Control (% EN) This control is similar to the balance control on conventional squarewave machines. But whereas conventional squarewave machines are limited to 68% EN, the Aerowave power source can be adjusted from 30% to 90% EN. Use the balance control in combination with the Independent Current Control for an even greater effect on EN.	*(waveform: EP+, EN−, Time)* (shown asymmetric)	More time in EN part of cycle: Deeper penetration and faster travel speeds	No Visible Cleaning / Bead Narrow bead, with no visible cleaning
	(waveform: EP+, EN−, Time) (shown asymmetric)	More current in EP than EN: Shallower penetration	Cleaning / Bead Wider bead and cleaning action

Figure 2.22 The asymmetric power source allows the operator to shape the arc and control the weld bead. Separately or in any combination, the user can adjust current control, frequency (Hz), and balance control to achieve the desired depth of penetration and bead characteristics for each application.

Note: All forms of AC create audible arc noise. Many asymmetric AC combinations, while greatly improving desired weld performance, create noise that may be objectionable to some persons. Hearing protection is always recommended.

Consult this chart when you are setting up an asymmetric AC TIG-welding machine. Especially note the two columns titled "Effect On Bead" and "Effect On Appearance" to decide which adjustment best suits your welding job. As always, practice on scrap pieces first. *Miller Electric Company*

MIG welding two pieces of 1/8-inch steel plate in a "T" shape is easy to do, but this is not high-quality welding. One tap with a hammer on the backside of the vertical piece and the weld will break.

CHAPTER SEVEN

MIG WELDING STEEL AND STAINLESS STEEL

High production rates and initial ease of operation make MIG welding attractive to many aircraft and race car builders. But, not everything is as it seems.

MIG welding is the most difficult of all manual welding processes to master.
— By Anonymous

The reasons that MIG welding is so hard to learn are numerous, and include

• The smoke and sparks made by MIG welding make it hard to see the seam to be welded.

• Once you squeeze the trigger, you are committed to weld at a fixed, unalterable speed.

• The weld puddle is hard to see because the gun nozzle is in the way.

• The welder must constantly aim the gun at the weld, meaning that the round tubes and anything but flat surfaces require lots of body English on the part of the welder.

• Choices of electrode wire make lots of difference in weld-ability and weld quality.

• Choices of shielding gas contribute to or detract from weld-ability and weld quality.

Now that I have told you about the problems with MIG welding, let me present some of the solutions:

• With better (more expensive) equipment, you can overcome most of the smoke and sparks, and you will be able to see the weld better.

• Many certified aircraft MIG welders have learned to give short, one- or two-second bursts of weld, thereby manually pulse-welding thin parts to prevent burn-through.

• You will be able to see the MIG weld puddle better if you look at the side of the weld so the gun

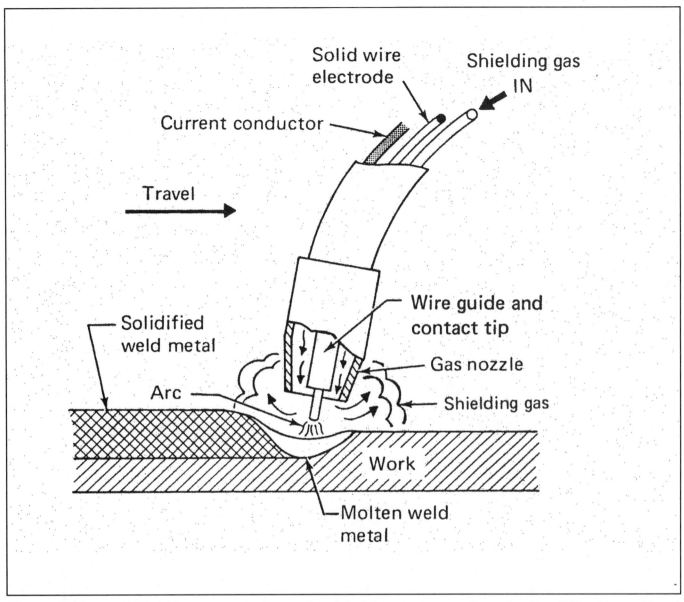

This drawing of a typical MIG-welding process helps illustrate the standard short-circuit arc transfer employed by a MIG-welding machine. *Lincoln Electric Company*

does not hide your view.

• For welding round tubing, you will need to practice moving your entire body around the tubing for better control of the weld, a solution to the statement above.

• MIG weld wire metallurgy is improving monthly. Stay in touch with the major manufacturers of MIG wire to be more sure of the best wire for the jobs you are doing.

• It appears that 75/25 gas (75 percent argon and 25 percent CO_2) is the best shielding gas for welding-steel, and argon-and-helium for welding aluminum. Stainless steel MIG welds require 90 percent helium and

7 percent argon plus CO_2. Again, no set, standard shielding gas is best for every welding situation. You will have to talk to welding gas dealers for the latest information.

Four MIG Processes

Before this chapter proceeds any further, we need to explain the four types of welding processes that are available with MIG welding. And you say that you thought there was only *one* kind of MIG welding? There are really four or more specifically different kinds.

The four basic MIG welding processes are:

• Short Circuit Transfer (the most common)
• Globular Transfer (used in heavy equipment)
• Spray Arc Transfer (for thicker metals, more penetration)
• Pulsed Spray Arc Transfer (for thinner metals)

Short Circuit Transfer

Most of the lower-priced MIG welding machines use this metal-joining process. In this process, a small-diameter wire is fed through a gun by an adjustable-speed electric motor, and when the wire touches the grounded base metal, an arc

Most MIG welders are easy to set up and operate. This midpriced machine has a spool of .030-inch wire and a drive roll adjustment inside the door. Nothing else needs attention.

It is okay to practice MIG welding on straight "T" joints, but almost anyone can master this technique in just a few minutes. Practice on tubular parts to learn faster.

A typical "T" joint welded with flux-core MIG wire. Flux-core leaves lots of slag and smoke that needs to be cleaned off.

starts and the wire melts off onto the base metal. This process occurs from 60 to 150 times per second, depending on how fast the wire is fed through the gun.

Short circuit transfer works with a flux-cored wire, a solid wire and shielding gas, and it works with steel, stainless steel, titanium, aluminum, and magnesium, as well as most other weldable metals. The welding arc with short circuit transfer sounds a lot like bacon frying in a pan.

Globular Transfer

In this MIG welding process, the welding wire short-circuits at the very start of the weld, but once the arc is established, the heat of the weld arc continues to melt globs of metal off the wire and into the hot weld puddle. The melted-off globs of metal are usually larger in diameter than the electrode wire diameter.

Globular transfer MIG welding is usually accomplished with the use of straight CO_2 shielding gas only, and higher voltages and amps than with short circuit transfer. Globular transfer MIG welding also produces more spatter beside the weld than short circuit transfer MIG welding, and it is mostly used in fabrication and repair of earth-moving equipment, where speed of welding is important.

Spray Arc Transfer

In this MIG welding process, a stream of tiny metal droplets are "sprayed" off the wire electrode into the weld puddle. These tiny droplets are usually smaller than the diameter of the welding wire. The arc is said to be on all the time once an arc is established.

The spray arc transfer uses a significantly higher voltage, higher wire feed speed, and higher amps than in short circuit transfer MIG welding. As a result, higher metal deposit rates are achieved. Because of the higher heat and higher wire feed speeds, the weld seam is usually wider, and that means that this process works best in the flat position, and for thick metals. Shielding gas mixtures are usually above 90 percent argon, with CO_2 and oxygen added.

Spray arc transfer welding is louder and much higher pitched than short circuit transfer welding and has a humming sound.

Pulsed Spray Arc Transfer

This could be the best kind of MIG welding for thin-wall tubing when all the characteristics get worked out. A special pulsed spray arc transfer welding machine must be used to dial-in the special output current, but the same machine will also weld the standard short circuit MIG welding.

In pulsed spray arc transfer, the special welding machine pulses the welding output to give high current peaks that are set at amp levels that cause the metal transfer to go into a spray. Then the background voltage is set at a level which will maintain the arc between the current peaks.

Because the heat input is lower, pulsed-arc transfer allows for welding thinner metals without heat distortion and without burn-through. In most cases, the shielding gas for this process is the same as for spray arc welding.

Lincoln Electric Company makes this push-button MIG welder that adjusts much like a modern kitchen microwave oven, with film switches rather than knobs or dials.

Which MIG Welder?

Remember that you are reading this book to become more proficient at *performance welding*. That means that you are not interested in making 50-percent-okay welds—you want to be able to make aircraft-quality welds in several kinds of metals. These requirements mean that you can't put up with bottom-of-the-line welding equipment.

Flux-core-only MIG welders would then be out of the question. Anytime you might save with flux-core MIG welders would be over-

shadowed by the time it takes you to chip off the flux and file off all the spatter that flux-core welding produces. And then you have to wire brush off the smoke that collects all over the weld.

Another problem with flux-core welding on small diameter thin-wall tubing is that every time you stop the weld and start again, you should chip off the flux and clean the weld so you won't bury flux when you start the weld again. On *one* tubular joint, this could be 20 to 30 stops and

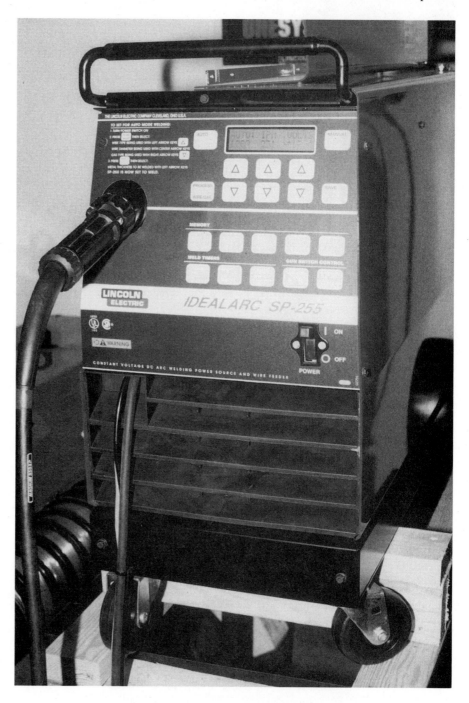

This Lincoln MIG welder has an added spot/stitch/seam timer feature that is handy for auto body sheet metal work, but it is not necessary for aircraft and race car welding.

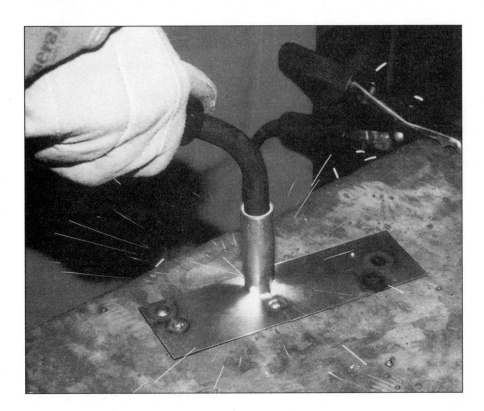

Tim Marr of Lincoln Electric Company demonstrates the spot timer feature that allows the operator to simply hold the MIG gun with a special four-slot cup against the metal and shoot pretimed welds.

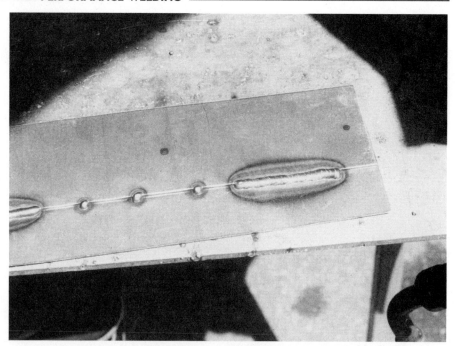

Sheet steel seam welds made by a MIG welder are fast and easy to do on flat plate, but trying the seam welds on thin tubing is a whole different talent to learn.

Tim Marr of Lincoln Electric Company demonstrates the proper two-hand method to accurately control the MIG gun when welding thin-wall tubing on a weld table.

Tim gets a good side-angle view of the tubing weld and prepares to do body-English to stay in viewing position while running the MIG weld bead.

starts before the weld is completed. I'll explain later in this chapter why you might start and stop that many times.

So, let's agree that the bottom-of-the-line flux-core-only welders are best suited to welding tee joints in 1/8-inch plate, and on a flat surface only. No uphill welding, no overhead welding, and for sure, no small round tubes.

How Much to Spend

To buy a good-quality, gas shield MIG welder that will weld all metals including aluminum, expect to spend about $1,800 to $2,500, somewhat more than you would spend for an equivalent TIG welding machine. The reason for this additional cost over the cheaper machines is that a machine that will accurately weld thick materials up to 5/16-inch thick

and down to .020-inch tubing will be microprocessor-controlled. In other words, computer-controlled.

CC CV Welders

There are several wire-feed welding machines that are just too powerful for delicate aircraft-quality welding. These 300-amp to 600-amp machines are a must for sky-scraper building and bridge welding, but using them for small work is similar to trying to drive a carpet tack with a 10-pound sledge hammer, you can't do a good job with oversized equipment. You can do a very good job on thin materials with a single-phase 220-volt, 250-amp machine. But, as with most things in welding, try the equipment before you decide on it. The most important factor in MIG welding thin

material is the ability of the welder to feed at slow rates, as low as 10 inches of wire per minute and amps of 20 or less. If the machine has a broad range of adjustments above those settings, that is good, too.

Wire Size

With most other kinds of welding, the welding rod should be about the same diameter that the weld part is thick. But not so in MIG welding. In MIG welding, the diameter of the welding wire electrode determines the amount of heat required to melt the wire into small drops of metal that make up the weld bead.

The smaller the wire diameter, the less heat it takes to melt the wire. The larger the wire diameter, the more heat it takes to weld and melt the wire. For

.035-inch wall thickness tubing, you need .023-inch diameter steel welding wire. If you are welding .750-inch-thick steel plates together, then .050-inch welding wire works better. Wire diameter is another variable in MIG welding. Therefore, it is a good idea to experiment with small, 5-pound spools of welding wire until you determine which size is best for your purpose.

Wire Alloy

There are more than 30 different MIG welding wire alloys, and the

A Bellanca Viking 300-horsepower airplane nose landing gear was factory MIG welded, and the somewhat thick, high weld bead is very evident.

reason for this large number of different metallurgical alloys is the attempt to improve starting characteristics and weld penetration characteristics. It is safe to presume, then, that soon there should be some metallurgical breakthroughs in determining the best wire electrode for welding 4130 chrome moly steel and stainless steel. In the meantime, study Chapter 12 and avoid the cheaper copper-coated welding wires.

Starting to MIG Weld

It is really easy to load a spool of

welding wire into most MIG welding machines. Just make sure that the free end of the wire is snipped off square and that there are no kinks to hang up when the wire is feeding through the hose, the liner, and through the MIG gun. Once the wire is passed through the drive rolls and into the liner, the trigger on the gun will feed the wire on through.

Once the wire is fed through the gun, back off the roller tension adjustment so there is no drag at all when the wire is manually pulled out

Aircraft-quality MIG welding is easy to spot in this Kitfox steel tube fuselage longeron and cluster weld

Another cluster weld on a Kitfox steel tube airplane fuselage shows the thicker-than-usual weld bead that clearly indicates MIG welding.

MIG welding is ideal for adding small, thin metal tabs to aircraft and race car tubular framework, because very little heat is needed to spot-weld small pieces. Oxyacetylene would require much more heat to fuse the tab to the tubular part.

This tack weld was obviously made with flux-core MIG wire. The slag needs to be chipped off before welding more.

Compare this tack weld to the one in the previous picture. This one was made with MIG and a 75/25 mix of gas shielding, leaving much less slag and smoke.

of the nozzle by hand. Then clip the excess wire off and make the proper tension adjustment.

To adjust for proper wire tension, put the nozzle against a nonconductive rigid surface, such as the cement floor of the shop. Next, squeeze the gun trigger with the machine turned on, and while holding the gun against the floor, begin to adjust the roller tension tighter until you feel the wire pushing the gun nozzle away from the floor. At that exact point, the tension is properly adjusted. Too loose and the wire will not feed; too tight and the rollers will wear out prematurely.

Aircraft Seat Welding

During the eight-year production run of Aerostar six-passenger aircraft at the Santa Maria, California, airplane factory, over 800 of the twin-engine executive airplanes were built, certified, and sold. Each airplane had six seats that were made by welding up 3/4-inch square 4130 steel tubing into seat frames. That means that over 4,800 steel frame seats were welded together during that eight-year period.

At first, the seats were TIG (heliarc) welded, but after building about 1,000 seats, with each seat taking 6 to 8 hours apiece to weld together, I decided to try building the

This practice MIG weld was made with flux-core wire, as is evidenced by the excessive flux and smoke.

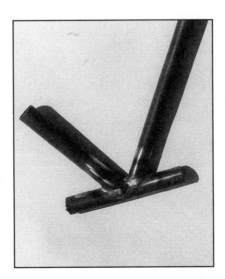

A typical practice weld using 75/25 argon/CO_2 gas leaves a large bead but no smoke or spatter.

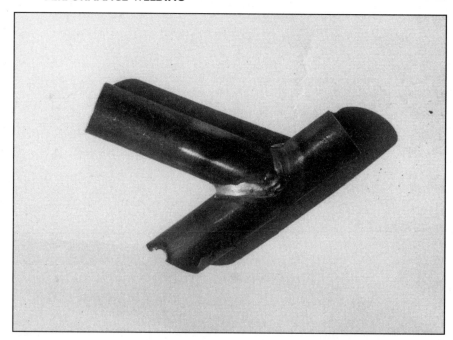

Practice your MIG welds on scrap pieces of tubing before starting your serious projects. The practice weld shown here is average and acceptable.

seats by MIG welding them to increase production.

A couple of our certified TIG welders volunteered to take the aircraft welding certification test by MIG welding the coupons. They passed the test easily and we began building seats out of .032-inch wall 3/4-inch square tubing. The first six seats built by MIG welding were tested to destruction by loading them in all directions from 9 gs to as much as 27 gs. None of the six seats failed any part of the test. It took considerably more loading to bend but not break the seats.

So we went into MIG welding production on the Aerostar seats and soon found that we could build four to six times as many seats in a given period as we could when we were TIG welding them. Therefore, our

Another practice weld on 7/8 x .035-inch wall tubing shows what can happen if you don't watch closely enough. This hole in the weld should be cut out, patched, and gas welded to repair.

conversion to the MIG process was a complete success, and it was a much faster process. MIG welding can be equally as effective in other aircraft welding production situations.

Stress Relieving

An important aspect of building more than 4,800 steel frame seats, both by TIG and MIG welding, is that we did not postheat stress relieve a single one of those seats. And not one of the seats ever developed stress cracks. I don't think we ever considered the age-old habit of oxyacetylene heating all the MIG and TIG welds to cherry- or blood-red after welding to supposedly stress-relieve the welds. Obviously, from the complete lack of postwelding cracks, we didn't need to reheat the seat frames.

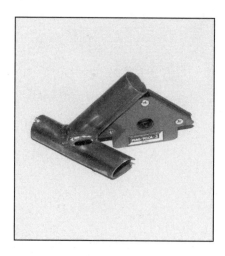

Conversely, if we had in fact tried the post-weld reheating process, we would have likely induced stress and caused cracks. Read Chapter 5 for additional information about stress-relieving after welding and the reasons you can't properly do it with an oxyacetylene torch.

MIG Welding Tips

For easier welding, you should

• Always weld in the flat position if at all possible, for better quality welds. This means not vertical, not horizontal, and for sure, not overhead.

• Never weld the "real" part until you have tested all the machine settings, amps, wire speed in fpm, gas flow, and especially test the weld accessibility.

• Always run a couple of test coupons on scrap material to make sure the machine settings and the operator are ready. Notice that the welder (operator) is a big factor.

• Always use anti-spatter spray or dip jelly to prevent spatter build-up in the gun nozzle.

• Be sure to protect painted surfaces from smoke and spatter from the weld.

• Never MIG weld where pets or people can watch the arc. Ultraviolet light is emitted from the arc, and ultraviolet rays can cause eye cataracts and skin cancer over a period of time. On a short-term basis, welding eye flash is painful. It causes late-night eye itching.

• Be sure to back up the weld seam with copper strips or welder's ceramic fiber paste when MIG welding stainless steel sheet, to prevent atmospheric contamination in the weld.

• Always back-gas purge the inside of the tubing when MIG welding stainless steel sheet tubing, to prevent weld contamination.

• Be your own automatic "stitch timer" when you are welding thin metal such as .020-inch to .050-inch thickness. Squeeze the trigger, weld a couple of seconds until you see a melt-through starting, then let up and let the weld cool and solidify for a couple of seconds, then squeeze the trigger and weld a couple of seconds more. Some of the biggest and best manufacturing companies weld tubular structures this way, with great results. Practice this procedure and you will soon develop the proper rhythm.

• Remember that dirt does not weld. Clean your parts properly before welding.

• Always keep the MIG gun cable from being twisted and tangled. Never stand on the cable while you are welding. The reason is that the wire inside the cable will not feed smoothly if the cable is twisted or if you stand on the cable.

Two basic controls adjust most MIG-welding machines. On this HTP welder, the bottom knob adjusts wire feed rate. You should adjust the amps knob for good heat and penetration and the wire feed speed for the smoothest arc, by sound.

The proper stance for starting a MIG weld. My helmet is up while I aim the gun, my left hand helps guide the gun, and my right hand is ready to squeeze the trigger.

The next step in starting a MIG weld is to nod your head, causing the helmet to fall in place. If you have an electronic lens helmet, you can aim the MIG gun with the helmet down.

• Change the cups and the copper collets often because dirty cups and worn collets reduce the quality of the weld.

• Never watch the weld from behind the MIG gun because you can't see the puddle that way.

• Always watch the weld from the side of the MIG gun, where you will be able to see the wire melt off in the puddle.

• Most important of all, never be embarrassed if you have to cut out a bad MIG weld because it is not sound. With a proper air-operated cutoff tool, it is not much trouble to cut out a bad weld on tubing. And then just redo it properly.

MIG Welding Stainless Steel

The same polarity setting that you used for welding steel is also used for welding stainless steel. That polarity is DCEP (DC Electrode Positive).

Three tack welds made with the HTP MIG welder hold the three tubes in place. Try this cluster assembly several times before you attempt to weld a serious project on an airplane fuselage.

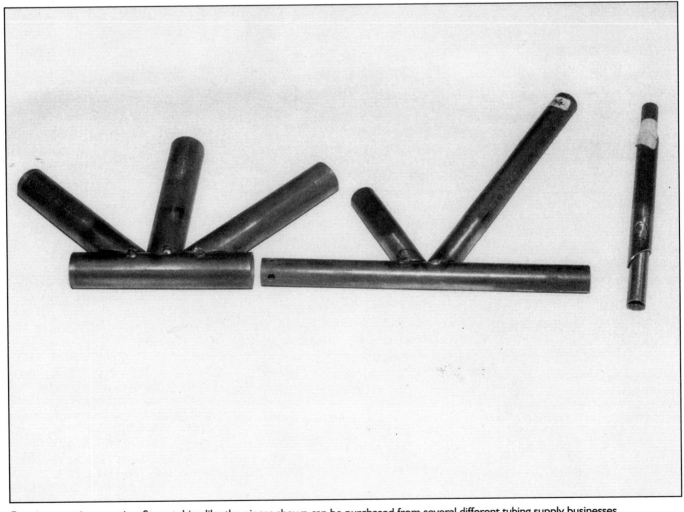

Practice, practice, practice. Scrap tubing like the pieces shown can be purchased from several different tubing supply businesses.

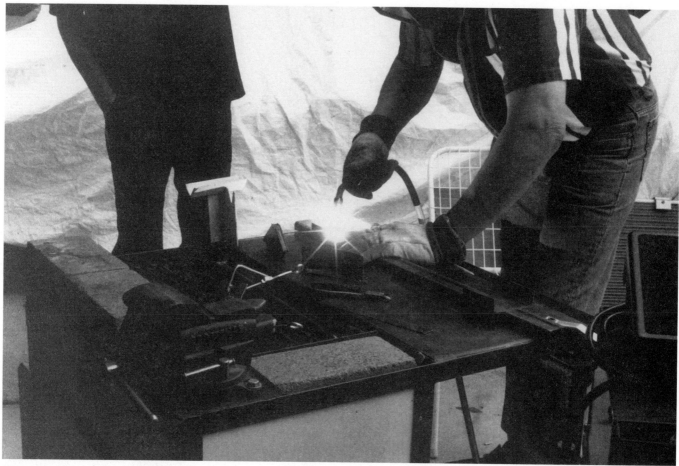

Here I am MIG welding a steel radiator brace for Patrick Lockwood's Griffin aluminum radiator in his 1964 Chevelle drag/street car.

The MIG gun is positive and the work is negative. The only time to change polarity when MIG welding is when you change from gas-protected to flux-core wire.

A noticeable effect of MIG welding stainless steel is that there will be considerable heat staining of the metal in the weld heat-affected zone. But there is a solution to the darkening of the stainless steel. Several companies make an acid-based cleaner that works very well. Use rubber gloves, of course, and with a cloth, wipe the weld down with the cleaner, then

Before welding anything serious, run a practice bead like this one to make sure the amps and wire feed speed are set correctly.

neutralize it with another cloth soaked in clear water. It comes clean like magic.

Back Side Protection

Stainless steel is very prone to crystallizing if it is exposed to air at welding temperature. Old welders call it "sugar" in the weld, meaning that the metal has crystallized, and when this happens, the weld is sure to crack sooner or later. The weld on the top side (front side) will look okay, but the back side looks like a tiny field of volcanic rocks. It is okay to make

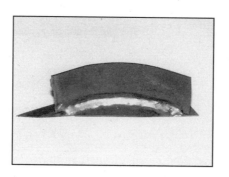

this happen on scrap pieces of stainless steel just to see how it looks and to break-test the weld to see how really weak it can be. But don't let this happen to good stainless steel parts. There are several ways to protect the back side of stainless steel welds from atmospheric contamination.

Back-Gassing

Say these two words to a certified aircraft welder or nuclear powerplant welder, and he or she will instantly know what you are talking about. You already know that you must have shielding gas on the welded side of your MIG welds to protect the metal from atmospheric (or air-oxygen and nitrogen) contamination. But the back side of the weld is also being heated to above the melting temperature, and therefore it must be protected to a level equal to the gas protection you have provided for the weld puddle.

Any inert gas works well for back gas-protection of stainless steel welds, but argon is the most common inert

This rolling chassis for a circle-track Chevy race car was MIG welded to speed up the fabrication time.

This Winston Cup Ford race car is actually a two-thirds scale Baby Grand Stocker that is powered by a four-cylinder motorcycle engine. The rolling chassis is MIG-welded mild steel tubing. *Baby Grand Manufacturing Company*

gas, and it is best to use this for back-gas purging. In a tubular assembly such as a stainless steel exhaust header assembly, simply close off all the openings with masking tape, put an argon hose in one end of the manifold and punch a pencil-sized hole in the other end of the manifold so the argon will flow through the pipe. Then purge for 5 to 10 minutes at 10 cfh flow.

To purge a flat seam, a copper heat sink plate with a half-round grove to flow argon through works very well. But in quick, one-time situations, a simple cardboard vee can be taped to the back side of the seam to provide an argon backing path for welding. Always make sure the argon flows all the way through the back-up dam and out the other end. Use flow rates of 5 to 10 cfh to back-gas purge.

MIG Welding Titanium

The data books give MIG wire numbers for titanium welding, but due to the fact that titanium is so prone to hydrogen contamination when it is being welded, the best way to fusion-weld titanium is in a vacuum chamber and with the TIG process. MIG welding titanium is a possibility, but it is an experimental process and welds should be tested before use.

Dye penetrant inspection testing is one way to test without damage to the metal assembly. Ultrasonic testing is another nondestructive testing method, and X-ray inspection is a third possibility.

Difficult Weld Process

At the beginning of this chapter, there was an anonymous quote that said that "MIG welding is the most difficult of all manual welding processes." I made that statement because there are so many variables in making the best-quality MIG welds in steel, stainless steel, and titanium. Unfortunately, you are not likely to be able to get good advice from the counterman at your local welding supply dealer, because he or she may have even less experience than you do. And a phone call to the home office of the American Welding Society will likely end up with a referral to some particular company that does a lot of MIG welding. But that is a better place to start researching the best gases and the best welding wire alloy for your particular job. Still, you may have to experiment to find the best process.

A new Baby Grand race car sits on a roll-around assembly table waiting for final assembly. *Baby Grand Manufacturing Company*

This is an excellent example of why MIG welding is *the* choice for many race car fabricators. The side-impact frame tubing has lots of inches of MIG weld seams. *Baby Grand Manufacturing Company*

Bare, powder-coated, MIG-welded race car frames sit on fabricated steel roll-around stands waiting for final assembly. *Baby Grand Manufacturing Company*

CHAPTER EIGHT

MIG WELDING ALUMINUM AND MAGNESIUM

My oldest son made his living for several months by MIG welding aluminum armor plate into West Coast type Fifth-Wheel trailers. MIG welding is completely adequate and very fast when welding truck toolboxes, diesel fuel tanks and brackets for trucks and tractors, and any other welding job where the aluminum is 1/8-inch thick or thicker. As a matter of welding history, some writers claim that MIG welding was first invented in order to weld aluminum more cleanly and much faster than by TIG or stick welding.

Although aluminum MIG welding is the real solution for welding truck bodies and other commercial equipment, it is not generally used for thinner aluminum such as aircraft nose cowling, fuel tanks, radiators, and other situations where the aluminum to be welded is less than .040-inch thick. TIG is the preferred method for thinner aluminum.

Weldable Aluminum

When it comes to the strongest weldable aluminum, 6061 is the highest strength at 45,000 psi in the T6 heat-treated condition. Next comes 5052 at 41,000 psi in the heat-treated condition, but 5052 provides only 29,000 psi tensile strength in the nonheat-treated condition. Lowest on the strength scale for weldable aluminum is 1100, almost pure aluminum at only 13,000 psi tensile strength.

Alloy 5052 aluminum is often used to make airplane fuel tanks and race car water expansion tanks because it forms better with less tendency to crack than 6061 aluminum. Although 1100 alloy aluminum is very easy to form and to weld, it is seldom used in aircraft or race car construction because it is too weak and dents easily.

A notable use of weldable 6061-T6 aluminum is the crew compartment on the four U.S. Space Shuttles. In order to pressurize a compound-curved structure the size of the Space Shuttle, welded seams in 6061-T6 aluminum were decided on as the best way to achieve a strong, leak-proof structure. Therefore, 6061

Aluminum MIG welding works well on thicker sections like this 1/8-inch plate welded to 1/8-inch wall tubing. A special MIG gun called a "Cobramatic" is used to ensure smooth wire feed right at the nozzle.

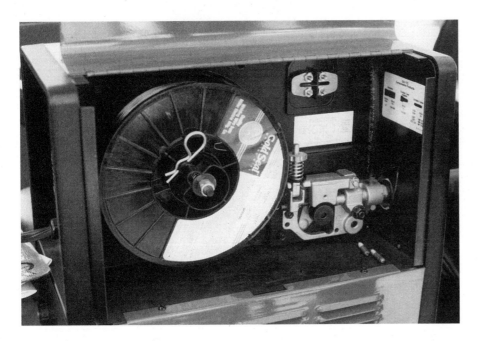

There are two U-shaped terminal tabs at the top of this 120-volt MIG welding machine. When the machine is used for flux-core wire welding, the tabs are positioned fore and aft as seen here. When aluminum welding with gas shielding, turn the tabs to 90 degrees, one above and one below. The machine is not an AC welder as in TIG welding.

aluminum is a good choice for weldable airplane and race car components.

Nonweldable Aluminum

Of the popular aluminum alloys, the two strongest alloys are not weldable. These alloys are 2024 and 7075. Yes, you can run a so-so weld bead on either of these alloys, but a significant crack usually follows the molten puddle to the extent that you can actually watch the metal crack within seconds of being welded, as the weld area cools. 2024 aluminum makes strong, formed and riveted or bolted structures. 7075 makes good, high-strength fittings, but don't try to weld them. The tensile strength of 2024-T4 is 68,000 psi. The tensile strength of 7075-T6 is 82,000 psi. A good rule to follow is that if a machined aluminum fitting has not been welded at the time of manufacture, it is probably nonweldable.

Heat Treating Aluminum

Often, it will be good to heat treat 5052 or 6061 aluminum parts after they have been fabricated by forming and welding. There are two methods for heat treating aluminum: solution heat treating and precipitation heat treating.

Solution heat treating is accomplished by dipping the aluminum parts into a bath of very hot brine solution and holding the parts in the hot brine for several minutes, depending on the mass (weight) of the part. After this 20-to 30-minute dip in hot brine, the part is immediately removed from the brine and dipped in cold water. The brine tank is usually 900 degrees F to 1,000 degrees F, and the cold water tank is usually below 50 degrees F.

Precipitation heat treating is accomplished by placing the aluminum part in a very hot oven, letting the part heat soak for a specified time, and then letting the part cure in still air that is 70° degrees F to 90 degrees F for another specified time period, usually 18 to 24 hours.

Heat treating aluminum cannot be properly done with an oxyacetylene torch because of the specific requirement for a thorough and long period of accurate heating. Consult the following charts to see what it takes to heat treat an average-sized airplane rib or bracket weighing less than 5 pounds.

If it becomes necessary to weld an aluminum part that was originally heat treated, it should be reheat-treated after welding to regain its strength. For instance, if you make a weld repair on a part that is 6061-T6, tensile strength of 45,000 pounds, welding it reduces its strength to as low as 18,000 pounds in the weld zone. It is true that it slowly regains part of its strength within 24 hours after it is welded; but the as-welded strength will be between 18,000 psi and 35,000 psi.

One sure way to determine the as-welded strength is to do a Brinnell ball indent test on the weld area. The deeper the small ball deforms the aluminum, the softer it is. Brinnell hardness testers are light and portable, and should be a part of every welding fabrication shop equipment where aluminum welding repairs are done. Several Brinnell testers I have used are about the size of a big pair of vice-grip pliers and operate in a similar manner by pinching the sheet metal between the jaws of the tester.

Aluminum MIG Welding Notes

Aluminum welding wire is much less stiff than steel or stainless steel MIG wire, and it kinks and tangles very easily. For this reason, it does not push through the average 10-foot-long MIG gun cable very well. But there are two solutions to this common problem:

1. Take out the wound steel core liners from your standard MIG gun cable and replace it with a special Teflon-lined cable liner that reduces the friction inside the cable. Most MIG gun and MIG welding machine manufacturers can supply special Teflon lines for their cables.

2. Another solution is to buy a special MIG welding gun that is called a *spool gun*. It has a drive motor mounted right on the gun so that aluminum wire will only be pushed 6 to 8 inches rather than 10 feet as with standard MIG welders. One well-known brand of spool guns is Cobramatic. Of course, the spool gun can only have small 2 1/2-pound to 4-

Solution Heat Treat Temps for Aluminum

Alloy	Temp °F	Quench	Temper
2017	950	Cold water	T4
2117	950	Cold water	T4
2024	950	Cold water	T4
6061	980	Cold water	T4
7075	875	Cold water	T4

Precipitation Heat Treat for Aluminum

Alloy	Temp °F	Aging Time	Temper
2024	æ	æ	æ
6061	325	18 hours	T6
7075	250	24 hours	T6

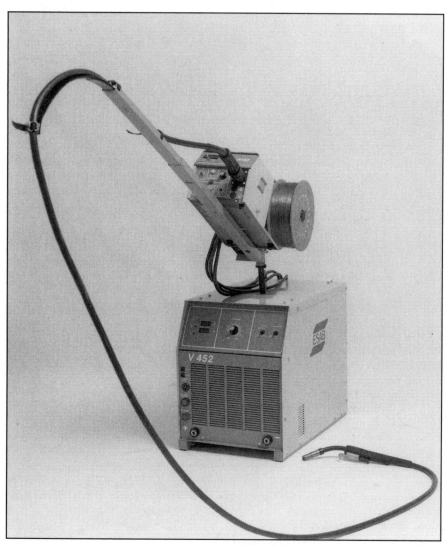

This large, heavy-duty, 400-volt commercial MIG-welding machine features a separate wire-feed module. *ESAB Welding and Cutting Products*

pound rolls of aluminum wire installed because a full-sized roll of wire would be cumbersome on the gun.

If you plan to do very much aluminum MIG welding, look into the possibilities of either a special Teflon liner for your standard gun or a spool-gun attachment.

Aluminum Coupons

One of the largest truck body manufacturers in the world uses MIG welding extensively in making permanent waterproof seams in the .050-inch-thick aluminum skins of their trailers. Their chief engineer specifies that no welds will be done without first running a set number of weld samples called coupons.

The reason for doing the seemingly extra work is that aluminum MIG welds can look good and can look fully integrated or penetrated into the base metal, when in fact the weld is just laying on top of the surface. The solution for this lack of fusion, of course, is to turn up the heat on the welder. The reason for *not* just turning up the heat as a matter of practice is that too much heat will burn (melt) holes in the aluminum, and holes in aluminum are time-consuming to repair.

In a factory situation, coupons can be tested in a special pull-test machine. In a small workshop situation, a suitable but less scientific testing method can be done. We call it "The Bench-Vise and Hammer Test." Just weld up your samples and put one end in your bench vise. Then, with a hammer, hit the sample on the other end, on the back side of the weld. If the sample can be bent 90 degrees toward the weld by hitting it with a hammer, and not crack or break, your weld is pretty good. If it breaks or ever starts to crack on the back side of the weld, you did not get sufficient penetration, because you needed to use more heat. So turn up the welding machine heat and make more test pieces. For aluminum MIG welding, a good size coupon would be 3- x 3-inch square, making a 3- x 6-inch coupon when it is butt- or seam-welded together.

This same coupon test process works for all other types of welding, too. Until you get familiar with your specific welding equipment and its performance, you should test your TIG welds and your gas welds this same way.

Aluminum Polarity

As you remember from Chapter 6, aluminum must be TIG welded using AC current and continuous high frequency for cleaning, or it can also be TIG welded with AC current that depends on square-wave technology.

But when you MIG (wire feed) weld aluminum, you don't use AC current. You use DC current, straight polarity, and you still use argon shielding gas. And because of the fact that aluminum oxidizes so fast, you can expect to have to flow more argon than usual to protect the weld from contamination. Rather than adjusting your flow meter for 20 cfh argon flow as you do when you are welding steel, you may need to adjust for 30 cfh to 50 cfh when you are MIG welding aluminum.

Aluminum Spatter

When you are MIG welding aluminum, you will notice that the gun nozzle picks up a lot more spatter than it does when you are MIG welding steel. Be sure to dip or spray the nozzle often when you are welding aluminum. After the first 30 minutes of welding, take the gun nozzle off and scrape the spatter out of the inside. If you neglected to coat the nozzle with spray or jelly, the spatter may stick permanently to the nozzle, making it necessary to replace it with a

Suggested Welding Alloys for Aluminum and Magnesium

Aluminum Alloy	Electrode	AWS Spec.
1100	ER1100 or ER4043	A5.10
3003,3004	ER1100 or ER5356	
5052,5454	ER5556 or ER5356	
6061-6063	ER4043	

Magnesium Alloy	Electrode	AWS Spec.
AZ10A	ERAZ61A	A5.19
AZ31B	ERAZ61A	
AZ80A	ERAZ92A	
ZE10A	ERAZ61A	
ZE21A	ERAZ61A	
AZ92A	ERAZ92A	
HK31A	EREZ33A	

Note: Read Chapter 12 for more detailed reasons to use a specific welding wire for MIG welding aluminum or magnesium.

new one. If you let spatter coat the inside of the nozzle, the argon gas cannot flow properly and your aluminum welds will start to turn black and sooty because of the lack of shielding gas protection.

Cleaning Aluminum

Do not try to weld dirty, oily, or paint-covered aluminum. It must be very clean in order to weld it properly. At the very least, clean all grease and oil off with acetone shortly before welding. You will also notice that aluminum oxidizes in the heat-affected zone even while you are welding. To remove this "instant oxidation," keep a small stainless steel wire brush handy and wire brush the weld seam area just before you start welding.

Back-Gassing

It is not necessary to back-gas purge thin aluminum while welding as is required when welding stainless steel, but using copper backup strips on the back side of the weld seam will prevent burn-through in most cases.

MIG Welding Magnesium

There are no special procedures for welding magnesium compared to welding aluminum. Extra care should be taken to weld magnesium in an area that is not flammable in case the magnesium catches fire. As you will read in Chapter 11 on welding safety, if magnesium catches fire, you cannot extinguish the fire with water or with any known fire extinguisher.

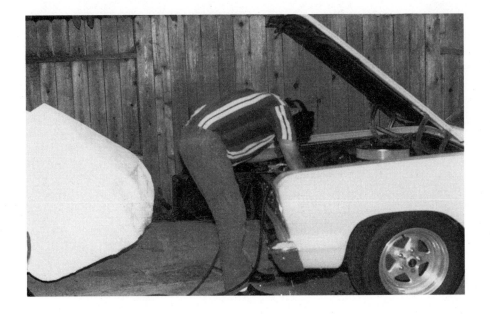

Here I am MIG welding a steel bracket in place for the aluminum radiator in Patrick Lockwood's 1964 Chevelle. The MIG machine is a 220-volt, gas-shield model that will also weld aluminum.

A typical example of heavy-duty oxyacetylene welding is this application of hard-facing metal to a 3/4-inch-thick steel plate. Regardless of the high-tech or low-tech aspects of a weld fabrication shop, *every* weld shop should have an oxyacetylene welding setup.

CHAPTER NINE

GAS WELDING STEEL AND STAINLESS STEEL

Gas welding (OFW or Oxy-Fuel Welding) is the basis for learning other, more modern kinds of welding, such as TIG and MIG. Learning to properly control the 6,300 degrees F heat of the flame to fusion-weld 4130 chromemoly steel which melts at 2,785 degrees F and vaporizes at 5,500 degrees F, is an art, just like playing a musical instrument. And like learning to play a musical instrument well, learning to gas weld well can be a satisfying talent to master.

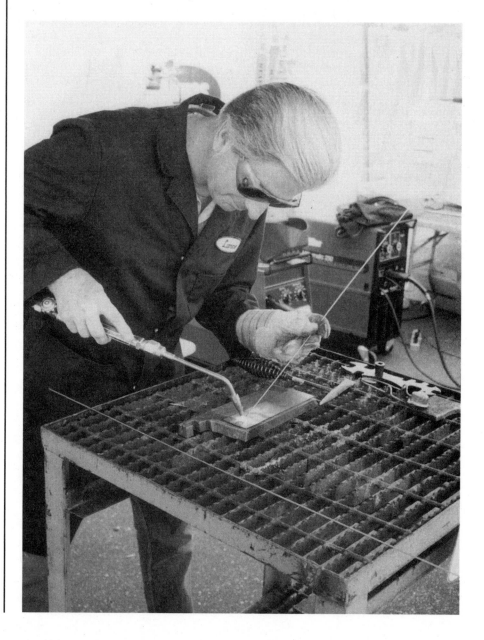

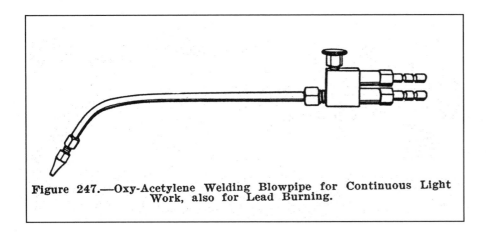

Figure 247.—Oxy-Acetylene Welding Blowpipe for Continuous Light Work, also for Lead Burning.

Oxyacetylene welding torches like this one were the only way to weld in the early 1920s. *Richard Finch Collection*

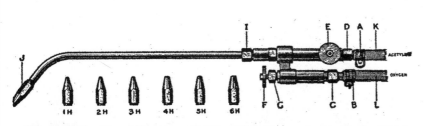

Figure 246.—Equal Pressure Welding Blowpipe. *A*, Clamp for Holding Acetylene Hose on Nipple; *B*, Clamp for Holding Oxygen Hose on Nipple; *C*, Union Nut on Oxygen Hose Nipple; *D*, Union Nut on Acetylene Hose Nipple; *E*, Needle Valve for Controlling Acetylene Supply; *F*, Needle Valve for Controlling Oxygen Supply; *G*, Stuffing Nut on Oxygen Needle Valve; *I*, Union Nut for Disengaging or Changing Angle of Barrel of Blowpipe; *J*, Interchangeable Welding Tip, Size 7H, 1H, 2H, 3H, 4H, 5H, and 6H are Extra Interchangeable Welding Tips.

A more complex oxyacetylene torch set from 1925 featured the same parts that are still in use going into the 21st century. This one just *looks* old. *Richard Finch Collection*

Beware of Obsolete Information

As I was reviewing several textbooks to make sure of facts regarding the latest information about gas welding, I was shocked to discover that a textbook reported to be the newest printing on the subject of gas welding (copyrighted in 1991) actually contained many reprints of articles written in 1935, 1940, 1953, and 1963. Metallurgically speaking, everything has changed since then. The information about welding filler metals and equipment in this chapter is the most recent, state-of-the-art information available going into the 21st century.

Same Basic Process

For the past 75 to 80 years, the physics of mixing equal parts of compressed oxygen and acetylene gas at 1 psi to 15 psi has produced flame temperatures of 6,300 degrees F, measured at the inner flame cone. The chemistry of the gases has not changed, and the process of consuming the two gases in a fire is still the same as it was in 1910 to 1920. The only factor that has changed is smaller, more accurate burning wands, or torches, as we call them today. Each manufacturer strives to make smoother operating and more dependable gas welding equipment so their product will sell better than their competitors' products.

In this chapter I have provided several pictures of early-day gas welding equipment to let you see the slow evolution of oxyacetylene welding equipment. Compare the old tools to what we have available today. The biggest changes are in the much smaller sizes of gas bottles we have now. The old equipment weighed over 300 pounds, and our new portable bottles weigh 25 to 30 pounds.

Starting Right

Several years ago, a friend asked me to stop by his house to help him with the gas welding of an engine mount for his plywood construction experimental airplane. As I pulled my car up in front of his garage, I saw him welding, with big pops of gas explosions, with sparks flying 10 feet or more in all directions. Remember that I said he was building a *plywood* airplane, so there was sawdust and wood scraps all over the floor, and the sparks were landing in all this flammable material!

God was lenient with him and, thankfully, his workshop, his airplane, and his house did not catch fire and burn to the ground! And I immediately saw his welding problem: His acetylene regulator was adjusted for 12 pounds pressure (15 psi is red-line) and his oxygen regulator was set at 25 pounds pressure. His excessively high gas pressures, combined with a very dirty welding torch tip, were conspiring to oxidize all his welds.

Once I cut his oxygen and acetylene pressures down to 4 psi and cleaned his welding tip, he was able to work pretty weld beads with no popping and almost no sparks coming off his welds. Within 10 or 15

Acetylene gas pressure for welding thin-wall 4130 steel tubing should be set at 4 to 6 psi.

Oxygen pressure should be set at the same number at which acetylene pressure is set for neutral-flame gas welding—about 4 to 6 psi, *not* higher.

This 4130 steel tube framework is laid out on a particle-board welding table for accuracy. Burn marks on the table are normal, and they indicate that another framework side has already been tack-welded on this table.

minutes, he had gone from a bad welder to a rather good welder, and I convinced him to sweep the floor and to have a water hose handy for possible fire extinguishing, just in case.

Gas Pressures

If your gas welding torch is in good condition (if it isn't by all means fix it), you should always weld with 4 psi to 6 psi gas pressures, both oxygen and acetylene. We use much higher oxygen pressures when we are cutting through 3-inch or 4-inch thick steel plate, because the cutting process is called an oxidizing cut. You can even cut thick steel plate with oxygen alone once the oxidizing cut has been started by oxygen plus acetylene. Just remember, too much oxygen pressure will oxidize your weld. Stick with low pressure for fusion welding steel.

Clean Your Tips

You should never begin a day or an hour of gas welding until you have thoroughly cleaned your gas torch

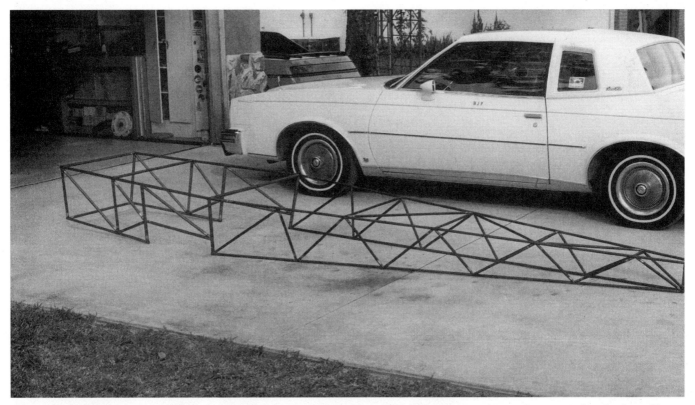

After two side frames are tack-welded, they are assembled on yet another weld jig with cross-members to form an airplane fuselage. After all the joints are tack-welded, the final welding takes place, starting at the front and working aft.

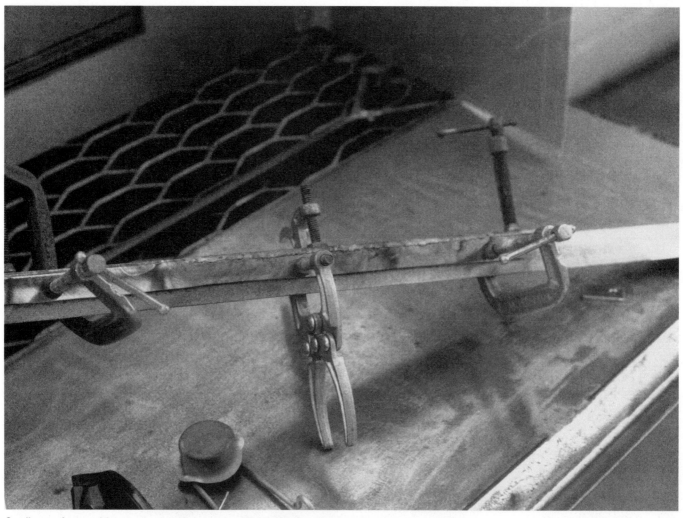

Small aircraft assemblies can be jigged up on a welding table with aviation clamps.

This 1930s biplane tail feather assembly clearly shows the extensive use of gas-welded steel tubing to frame the lightweight structure.

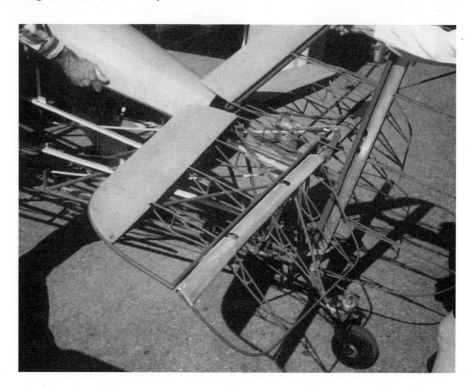

welding tips. Every time you weld, there are tiny and sometimes large sparks that fly up from the molten weld puddle. These sparks are really red-hot pieces of metal, and they stick to every piece of metal they touch, including the inside and outside of your copper welding tips.

First, ream out the inside of the tip with the largest wire reamer that will easily fit inside the tip. Next, scrape the outside of the tip to remove all carbon and slag that is sticking to the tip. Then, carefully file the opening area of the tip to remove the slag that is still sticking to the end of the tip. Finally, I usually wipe the outside of the tip with my acetone cloth that I clean the welding rod with. If you have shop air, you can blow out the inside of the tip.

The reason you should always start off by cleaning the welding torch

tip is that all that slag that sticks to the tip acts like a heat collector and makes the tip heat up more than usual, causing the torch to pop.

Causes of Popping

Being a self-taught welder, I admit that I welded lots of race car frames and parts over a period of 15 or more years before I finally figured out why gas torches pop and how to prevent the popping. I'll tell you so you can get past this problem and do much better welds without the dangerous nuisance.

Oxyacetylene torches pop because they are overheated. They become overheated for several reasons, including

• When you are using a tip that is too small for the work you are welding, you keep putting the torch closer to the metal in order to make a good

puddle, and then the heat from the weld reflects back to the torch body, causing it to overheat. When the torch tip overheats, the gases inside the tip will explode (the pop), causing welding sparks to fly all over the place. This is a dangerous situation.

To solve that problem, change to the next size larger tip. Sometimes you have to go two or three sizes larger to stop this overheated popping.

• Another reason for occasional popping of the torch is just a dirty tip. Look at the tip, and if it has slag stuck to the last 2 or 4 inches of the tip, stop welding and clean the tip.

The reason that dirty tips tend to pop is that the dirt/slag on the tip collects heat a lot faster than a clean, new tip does. It actually helps to sand the tip to its natural copper color to reduce popping. Some welders spray MIG welding antispatter on their gas

This biplane was built by gas welding mild steel tubing into an airplane structure. The left landing gear leg attachment is shown here.

The firewall side of the airplane's engine mount is a good example of how a sound gas weld should look when it is finished and painted. Note that the weld bead is three or four times wider than a TIG weld.

This gas-welded structural longeron fitting is the minimum quality you should try for. The welder who made this weld was very nervous!

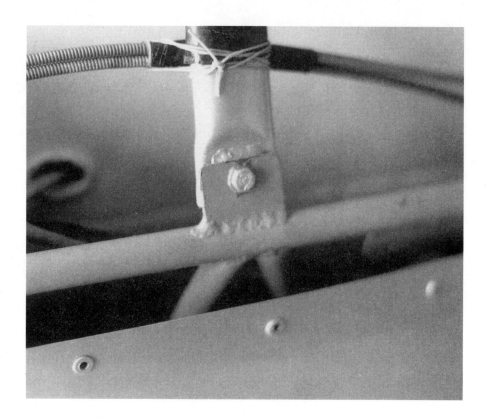

One of the world's best aerobatic show biplanes is this 200-horsepower Pitts S1-A that was built by gas welding its 4130 steel fuselage and 4130 steel tail.

welding tips to reduce spatter build-up, and that solution works well also.

• If you are welding into a corner, the flame and heat will be reflected back toward the tip. Again, overheated tips contribute to torch popping. If this is the cause of popping, change the torch angle to make it reflect less heat back on you and the tip. If that is the cause of popping, the problem will go away.

• If your welding tip is badly worn, it will not produce a symmetrical flame. A crooked or badly shaped flame will not produce the proper heat, and the torch will always pop, no matter what you do. If your favorite torch tip has been used for more than five years, it is probably worn out. Buy a new tip and see if your welding improves.

Neutral Flame

One thing that is consistent with most welding textbooks is that they usually show drawings of three different oxyacetylene welding flames. The three flames are *oxidizing* (too much

oxygen), *carburizing* (too much acetylene and soot), and *neutral* (equal pressures and equal amounts of both gases). You should know by now that there is no welding job that requires an oxidizing flame or a carburizing flame. A neutral flame is the only flame for gas welding.

Adjusting for a neutral flame is easy. You start by turning the acetylene valve on the torch to about one-third to one-half turn open and light the torch with a flint striker (not a butane lighter!). As soon as the acetylene flame lights, quickly open the oxygen valve to about one-third turn. At that point you will have almost a neutral flame, but continue to adjust the oxygen and acetylene valves until the inner flame core just becomes a single flame.

Three Flame Sounds

With one particular size welding tip, you can adjust the flame for three different heat ranges, judged by three different sounds. Those three sounds are a soft, whisper flame; a medium

sound; and a noisy, rather hissing flame. The inner cone of all three of these flames is still 6,300 degrees F temperature, but the BTUs, or volume of heat, is different for each flame.

It works better to braze and weld very thin material with a soft flame. The medium flame works well for fusion welding materials such as exhaust pipe tubing and 4130 chromemoly structures. The noisy, hissing flame is a partial solution when welding thicker materials such as angle brackets, usually from mild steel. At no time should you try to weld important, "life supporting" parts with a loud, hissing flame because the actual flame pressure tends to boil and misform the metal. Just change to a welding tip one or two sizes larger to eliminate the need for a really loud flame.

Gas Welding Sparks

There will always be a few intermittent sparks that come out of the weld puddle when you are properly gas welding steel. These sparks are tiny, and they seldom go more than 12 inches before they die and go out.

If you are getting a constant shower of sparks with some that fly 5 to 10 feet away from your weld puddle, stop welding and fix this obvious problem. That many sparks indicate that you are burning and boiling the metal. You are making weak, crystallized welds. Quite likely, you need a tip that is one size larger and a softer flame. It may be that you even need a tip two sizes larger. Try it and see which works best.

If the part is an important part, you should inspect the weld closely and consider cutting out the bad weld bead with an air cut-off wheel. Then start over and do the weld right. One big difference in gas welding today, compared to 25 to 50 years ago, is the invention of air

I restored the rusted tubes in this 1930s Army trainer glider by welding in new splices to replace the bad tubes which were mostly in the bottom part of the fuselage. Interestingly, the rust was from the outside; there was no linseed oil inside any of the tubes.

Here is an excellent example of a gas-welded stainless steel exhaust system on a 1939 Army Birddog observation airplane, made by Piper Aircraft Company. Notice that the pipe was made from formed sheet, with two halves gas welded together.

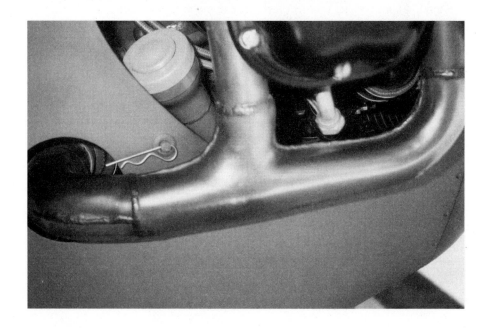

tools. Welds that can be cut out in 30 seconds with an air cut-off wheel would have taken 15 minutes to saw and file out in 1940.

Gas Welding Tubular Frames

Take a close look at the pictures in this chapter and copy the particle-board welding table for large framework projects. A picture *can* be equal to a thousand words of written instruction. This type of low-production frame assembly is a time-proven one, and it works well. Copy it, and your project will work well.

Learn by Looking

I have provided several pictures in this chapter of aircraft-quality welds that are not perfect, but they are acceptable. Go out to the shop and set up some practice welds to get the feel of how the sample welds were done. After you have completed a few welds, inspect them and compare them to the pictures of gas welds in this chapter. With just a little practice, you will be able to weld as good as any of the welds pictured here.

Welding is an acquired art. When you are learning to make good air-craft-quality welds, think about what you are doing. Think about the exact time to dip the rod into the puddle to make the fitted seam one continuous, smooth piece of metal. And then gas-weld each tubular joint one dip of the welding rod at a time.

Common Gas Welding Mistakes

For absolute beginners at gas welding, the common mistake is trying to melt off pieces of the welding rod and drop the melted pieces onto the seam, hoping the parts will glue themselves together. Even advanced

Oxyacetylene brazing is being done here by a welder who is using flux-covered brazing rod.

welders still try to heat the welding rod. But you will never learn how to weld if you persist at melting the welding rod.

The secret to good gas welds is to slightly preheat the weld area with the torch flame, then concentrate the flame where *you* want the first tack weld to be. Then, if your tip size is correct, within three to five seconds you should see a molten metal puddle forming on both pieces of metal to be welded. At that instant, dip the welding rod into the area where the puddle has formed, then pull the rod back out.

You have just deposited one drop of weld rod into the weld. Then, each time you dip the rod into the puddle, a drop will melt off and flow into the weld, forming a weld bead. Maybe you can think of forming a weld bead as being similar to knitting a sweater. In knitting, each time you grab the knitting yarn, you make a stitch. Soon, with a consistent pattern you

will have a knitted sweater. And soon, if you keep a consistent pattern of forming and maintaining a puddle and dipping the welding rod into it, you will have a beautiful weld seam.

Another mistake that new welders make is burning holes in their welds. Good, tight fit-ups will do a lot toward preventing holes in the welds, but if one starts to melt in front of you, immediately pull the torch back 2 or 3 inches to reduce the heat on the weld. Then go back and quickly put weld rod material at the edge of the hole to cool it. Yes, welding rod cools the weld puddle. Usually you can fill small holes with welding over them, but if they get bigger, stop welding, cool the weld by waiting a couple of minutes, then make a small patch to cover the hole, and include the patch in your weld.

There is no fixed size to tell you when to make a patch over a hole, but use good judgment and don't weld a patch so small that it melts before you

can weld it into the structure. My rule of thumb is that a melted hole the diameter of a pencil needs a patch three times the diameter of the hole you are patching. Once you patch a hole, you will try a lot harder to avoid burning holes in the future. And again, a tightly fitted tube is a lot less likely to melt into a hole.

Bending Tubing

The most simple tubing benders are the electricians' conduit "Hickeys." You can buy three of four sizes of these manual conduit benders at your local builder's supply outlet. Most of these benders have a provision for screwing in a pipe handle. These benders work fairly well for putting mild bends (just a few degrees) into 1/2-inch, 5/8-inch, 3/4-inch, 7/8-inch, and 1-inch thin-wall 4130 steel tubing. They are designed to put 90-degree bends into EMT thin-wall electrical conduit. But they will collapse the wall of 4130 steel

This is Saturday morning of a weekend race-car-building project. I have bent the tubes, notched them to fit tightly, and I am preparing to braze them together.

This is Sunday afternoon on the weekend race-car-frame-brazing project, without any helpers. This point in the frame project represents about 20 hours of bending, fitting, and brazing.

tubing if you try to put too tight a bend in it.

There are several other types of tubing bending machines that can do a good job of bending aircraft quality tubing, but these hydraulic benders sell for $500 or more. If you are doing production bending, it might pay to invest in one of these benders, though.

Another bender that works well for small jobs is a three-roller adjustable bender. I have seen these bend 1-1/4-inch diameter stainless steel tubing into circles small enough to make a yacht tiller wheel—about 18 inches in diameter. That would be a 9-inch radius bend. Many shops make their own roller benders. The important thing is that each of the three rollers must be radiused to fit the tubing snugly to prevent the sides of the tube from spreading out and kinking. That means that each diameter of tubing you want to bend must have a special set of three roller dies to fit it. I have even bent 3-inch diameter .090-inch wall stainless steel tubing to a 200-inch radius with one of these homemade tubing benders.

Another solution for one or two tubing bends such as might be needed for a race car roll bar or an airplane windshield bar would be to take your tubing to a commercial tubing bending shop in your locality. In any event, you ought to have a full-sized drawing of your desired bends. *Do not try to bend thin-wall tubing by*

heating it. Try it once and you'll quickly know why!

Rust Protection

For many years, welders were told to fill the inside of each welded tube in an airplane fuselage with linseed oil to prevent rust. Now, just imagine for a couple of minutes what would happen in a year or two when the tube developed a crack: The linseed oil would leak out all over the airplane fabric and ruin it.

And what if you decided to weld on a couple of small radio antenna brackets after the fuselage frame was completed and painted? All that linseed oil inside the tubes would likely catch fire, and it might even explode! So, do *not* fill your welded steel tube structure with oil to prevent rust. That is a silly thing to do.

I have repaired a large number of welded airplane structures that were built from 1930 through 1960, and none of them had linseed oil inside the tubes. If the welds are solid, moisture will not get inside the tubes to cause rust. Any rust that might form will be from moisture on the outside of the tube, not inside the tube.

Companies that weld tubular frames these days explain that they believe the manufacturing oil that comes inside and outside new 4130 steel tubing is sufficient rust protection if you leave it inside the tubes and don't rinse it out with solvent. We just

now debunked another of the "old welders' tales" about rust protection!

Gas Welding Stainless Steel

It is entirely possible to make pretty, strong, sound welds on stainless steel with an oxyacetylene torch. To see what those welds look like, take a look at the picture of the 1939 Piper Army Birddog observation plane exhaust pipe in this chapter.

The secret to making sound gas welds like the ones in the picture was to add a flange at the weld seam to keep the weld heat off the main part of the pipe. Because the flange sticks up, it is easy to heat it to its melting point without heating up the rounded part of the pipe. It is possible to add exactly the right-sized flange so that the flange will be melted down to almost flat when the weld is completed.

There are a few companies that have been in business many years, furnishing flux for gas welding stainless steel. Check Chapter 12 for sources of stainless steel welding flux.

Back Side Protection

As with TIG and MIG welding of stainless steel, it is important to protect the back side of your oxyacetylene welds on stainless steel. You can even use a small argon bottle and a flow meter to argon-purge the back side of your gas welds. It works the same with gas welding as it does with arc welding. If you don't have a suit-

The race car frame in this picture is 99-percent brazed mild steel tubing, including the suspension A-frames.

able setup for argon purging, at least use one of the ceramic paste products listed in Chapter 12 to improve your stainless steel gas welds.

Stainless Steel Colors

Unlike chromemoly steel, stainless steel does not produce the same color changes during the welding process. It does go from silver color at room temperature to black at 1,000 degees F, to dark red just before it begins to melt at 2,600 degrees F. Stainless also starts to produce a black scale when it is heated to 1,600 degrees F. This black scaling is the primary reason for using flux when gas welding. Flux cleans off the scale, preventing weld contamination. This scale is like ashes, and it has no strength. Keep a small stainless steel wire brush handy to clean the weld.

Brazing Steel

Always avoid brazing 4130 steel. The reason to not braze chromemoly is that this steel has a definite grain structure that actually opens up at medium red brazing temperatures. When brazing alloy is melted onto the steel surface, it flows easily into the many small cracks and crevices in the chromemoly steel. Then, as the braze joint cools, the brass will not compress and it forces major cracks to form in the 4130 steel. Often, a brazed 4130

steel part will crack completely in two before your eyes as it cools.

Mild steel (1020, 1025, and so on) is ready-made for brazing. It does not have the same kind of grain structure that 4130 steel does, and therefore it will not crack when brazed at the correct temperature. The correct brazing temperature for mild steel is 1,250 degrees F to 1,350 degrees F, which is a blood-red to cherry-red color. Any hotter and you will begin to boil the brass brazing rod (not filler rod).

Look at the pictures in this chapter that show brazed race car frames. They are fitted exactly the same as a fusion-welded 4130 steel frame would be fitted, meaning no open joints and no wide gaps. By its nature, brass brazing rod loves to flow into seams measuring from .001-inch to .005-inch wide. Any wider and the capillary action of molten brass does not work. Keep your brazing joints as tight as possible.

Chapter 12 will give you suggestions for the best brazing rod for mild steel, thin-wall tubing. Be sure to note in the brazing rod specifications that the tensile strength of most brazing rod is 90,000 psi, which is stronger than the 60,000 psi mild steel that you braze with it. Brazing, when done correctly, can last as long as any other metal-joining method. And it can be as strong as fusion welding when it is done correctly.

To clean off the flux after the brazed joint is cool, use warm water to soften it, then wire brush it to remove the white flakes. A warm water-soaked rag works well for cleaning flux off a tubular frame structure.

Brazing Drawbacks

Brazed joints can be weak if too little rod is used to make the joint. If you make sure to build up a good fillet of brass on the joint, this will not be a problem. Brazing is not strong enough to use for butt joints. Always make sure to provide for a fillet of brazing material to ensure a strong joint. The flux residue that adheres to the braze joint after the metal cools is a nuisance. If you don't clean it off completely, it will continue to slowly flake off, even years later. If the part you brazed will fit in a water tank, soak it in warm water for 15 minutes after brazing and then the flaky flux will simply wire brush off.

Stainless Steel Brazing

For many stainless steel assemblies, brazing can be a completely adequate process, and the brazed joint will be stronger than the stainless steel base metal. But not just any brazing rod will work on stainless steel. You need a high silver content brazing material to stick to stainless. Again, check Chapter 12 for the best brazing rod to use on stainless steel.

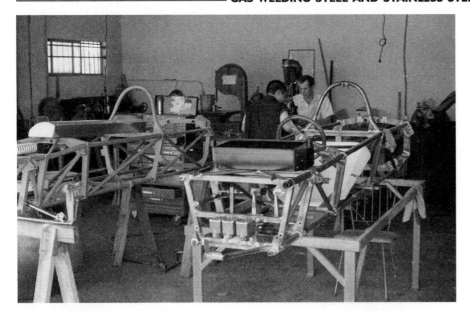

The LeGrand Formula Ford race car factory brazed these mild steel tubing Formula Ford frames because brazing is a stronger and faster fabrication method than fusion welding.

The completed race car frame, minus the lightweight fiberglass body, required 12 months of part-time work to complete.

Special gas-welding lenses called "Cobalt Blue" are much better for welding aluminum than the standard green tint lenses. Specify a number 3 tint lens. Also shown in this picture is a prescription-ground lens made for welding goggles.

CHAPTER TEN

GAS WELDING ALUMINUM

I dislike the phrase "best kept secret," but that is a good phrase to describe the mysterious (to many people) process of gas welding aluminum. I have found that most books that advertise to teach you how to weld aluminum merely tell about the obsolete alloy identification numbers such as 2S, 3S, and other useless information. Next, they tell how to weld thick pieces that have to be V-grooved with three or four weld passes. They say nothing about how to weld aluminum hoods on cars, aluminum nose cowls on airplanes, or aluminum nose cones on older race cars. So, I will tell you those untold things in this chapter.

Gas Welding Limits

Any aluminum welding projects that include metal thickness over 1/4-inch or under .050-inch should not be gas welded. Sure, it is possible to gas weld thicker or thinner aluminum than these limits, but it is better done with TIG welding. It is possible to tack-weld your parts together and then take them to a commercial welding shop for finish TIG welding, but it would actually be easier to simply jig the parts so the TIG welder can weld everything without worrying about heat distortion from tack welds. Each project should be evaluated individually, but as an example, if I wanted to build a 5/16-inch 6061-T6 plate gearbox housing for an auto engine conversion, I would not even try to gas weld that project. But if I needed to weld up a 1/8-inch 6061-T6 engine mount bracket for a racing go-kart, I would expect to do that gas welding project with little problem. The only way that you are going to be able to decide your own personal aluminum gas welding limits is to practice welding on pieces of scrap aluminum.

Equipment Required

A standard oxyacetylene torch setup and a gas welding green eye goggle will work okay for welding aluminum. Chapter 12 of this book will give you numbers and names of aluminum welding rod suppliers. You also will need a jar (not a can) of aluminum welding flux.

But while oxyacetylene will work, the ideal setup for gas welding aluminum is an oxyhydrogen gas set and a cobalt blue lens for your welding

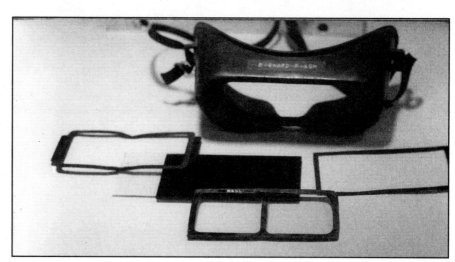

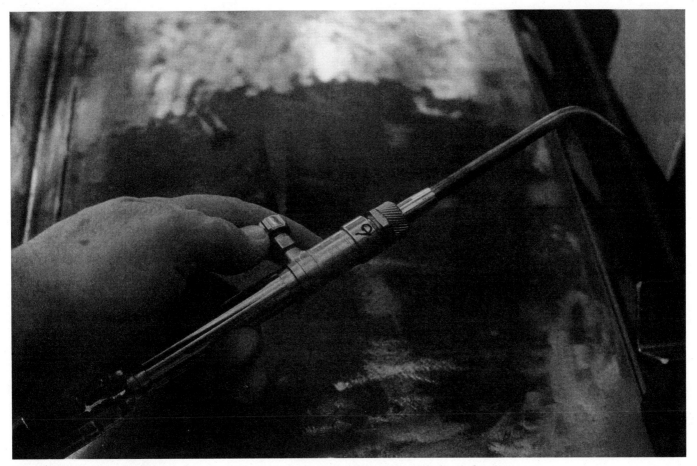

This Smiths aircraft-sized torch works very well for welding aluminum. The torch weighs barely 9 ounces.

goggles. The reason that hydrogen gas works better than acetylene gas is that hydrogen burns with a mostly colorless flame. You will therefore be able to see the weld puddle better and you will be able to better control the fusion process.

The reason for changing to a cobalt blue welding lens is that a blue lens filters out the bright yellow light coming off the weld, again helping you see the puddle better. Even if you must use acetylene rather than hydrogen, the blue lens will make your aluminum welds much easier to see, and therefore easier to make.

Hydrogen Gas

If you plan to gas weld aluminum on a regular basis, you can set your shop up for oxyhydrogen welding. You will also need to keep an acetylene setup for welding steel because hydrogen and steel welding don't mix. Hydrogen in steel welds causes hydrogen embrittlement and cracks in steel welds.

You will need to purchase a second high-pressure gas regulator and gauges, like the one you already use for your oxygen bottle. You should not use your oxyacetylene hoses because you need a hose setup with both hoses for right-hand threads. Or you can convert the second high-pressure regulator to acetylene-type left hand hose fitting threads, but if you do, put a permanent tag on the regulator that says "Hydrogen Gas Only" so you don't try to hook it up on your oxygen tank by mistake.

Of course, you will also need to lease or buy a high-pressure hydrogen tank, filled with hydrogen gas. Always remember to treat compressed hydrogen as a very flammable and potentially explosive gas. The thing about hydrogen is that it burns clean with no residue, but it could explode "clean" if heavy concentrations of vapors are ignited.

You do not need to make any changes to your gas torch in order to burn oxy-hydrogen in equal amounts

for welding aluminum. Because aluminum requires more heat to preheat for welding, you should use one size larger tip than for welding the same thickness steel.

Oxy-Hydrogen Flame

You will need to adjust the oxy-hydrogen welding flame exactly the same way you adjust an oxyacetylene flame: Open the hydrogen valve on the torch first (with 4 to 6 psi pressure) and light a flame with a spark-type striker; then open the oxygen valve at 4 to 6 psi pressure, and adjust for a neutral flame.

The flame will be nearly colorless, but you will be able to see a faint inner flame cone that is burning at 5,400 degrees F rather than at 6,300 degrees F as with acetylene. And once again, before you attempt to weld a real project with oxy-hydrogen, practice on several pieces of scrap aluminum until you get the feel of how the hydrogen flame reacts on the metal.

Real Projects

My first two self-taught aluminum gas welding projects were for racing go-karts. First I welded up a butterfly-shaped steering wheel from 1/4-inch aluminum plate and 1- x .049-inch aluminum tubing. Next, I welded up a 1/8-inch 6061-T6 plate engine mount. Both projects stayed together although the welds were rather lumpy and ugly.

There was only one secret to making good welds in aluminum. That secret was that there was no tell-tale color change in the aluminum as it reached its welding temperature of 1,250 degrees F. It only changed from dull to shiny just before a puddle formed. Aluminum does not exhibit color changes as it is heated from room temperature to melting temperature. Learn this simple fact, and you will be well on your way to becoming proficient at gas welding aluminum.

Flux

Aluminum oxidizes (the equivalent of rusting) as it is heated. The only way to remove this oxide film is to completely bathe the weld seam with a flux that will inhibit and effectively prohibit oxides from forming. I have become partial to flux-core aluminum welding and brazing rod. I have found that no extra flux is needed for most aluminum welding jobs when using this rod. The only negative thing about flux-filled aluminum brazing rod is that it has a bond strength of 28,000 psi, but it does have a tensile strength of 50,000 psi. One of the good points about using flux-cored aluminum brazing rod is that it has a high melting point of 1,080 degrees F to 1,100 degrees F, which means it will stand as much heat after welding as the base metal aluminum does at 1,217 degrees F temperature.

Separate aluminum welding fluxes are also available. Usually you mix these dry powder fluxes with water or denatured alcohol to form a liquid paste that can be brushed on the base metal and on the aluminum welding rod.

Parent Metal Rods

When aluminum welding car bodies, fenders, hoods, and trim was

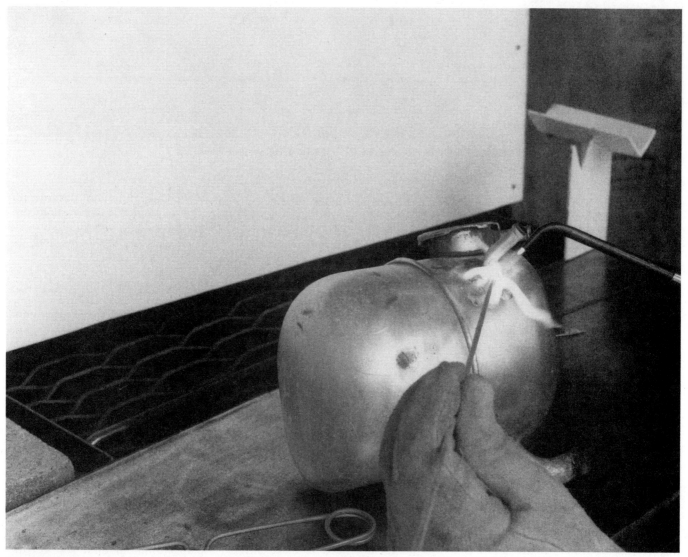

Using the Smiths torch and a small tip with a soft flame, I am repairing a loose tube in this Corvette radiator overflow tank that is made of 5052 aluminum.

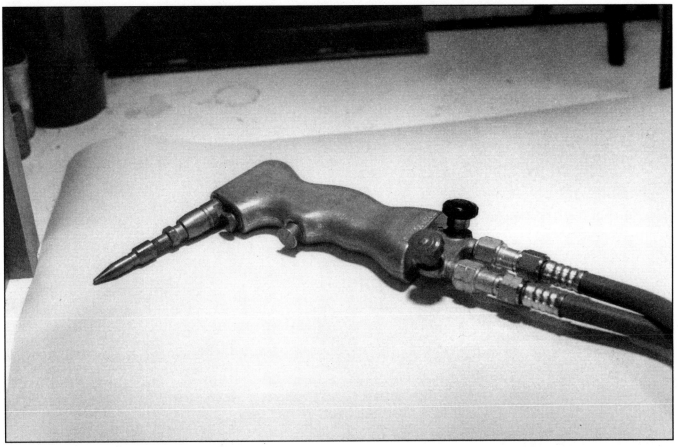

Another type of gas-welding torch is this Dillon/Henrob unit that weighs 32 ounces; it's three-and-a-half times heavier than the Smiths torch, but it produces a more pencil-tip flame for delicate aluminum welding. It also has flashback arrestors at the torch adjustment valves.

common, back in the 1930s, the only way to find a positively compatible welding rod was to shear off a narrow strip of the actual aluminum sheet that was to be welded. If the metal was S2, 18-gauge, then you had a piece of S2, 18-gauge welding rod to use. And, of course, you needed lots of flux and a good stainless steel bristle wire brush to clean your welds. This method is still workable for welding aluminum. The problem with it is that you first must have a spare sheet of the correct weldable aluminum, and you must have a 4-foot-wide metal shear that will accurately shear off thin strips of that sheet aluminum. Tin snips can be used to cut thin strips if necessary; however, with modern metallurgy, this time-honored aluminum welding procedure is no longer really necessary. You can just go to a welding supply and buy a few sticks of appropriate aluminum welding rod. Read Chapter 12 for accurate information about aluminum welding rod.

Now, the Procedure

Here is the part you have been waiting for: how to gas weld aluminum and magnesium!

1. Brush the flux paste on the weld seam area, but only about 4 inches of length at a time.

2. For thin butt welds, clamp a copper backup strip to the back of the weld so you won't burn holes in the aluminum sheet.

3. For just five or six seconds, bathe the weld torch flame on the weld joint to slightly preheat the aluminum. Be sure you have flux paste on the seam.

4. Now, you are ready to weld. Point the torch at the weld with a 45-degree angle to the seam, not 90 degrees as with steel welding.

5. The second that you see the aluminum get shiny and start to melt, immediately dip one or two drops of aluminum weld rod into that shiny puddle, then pull the rod back out *and* pull the torch back an inch or so to cool the weld.

6. Then keep repeating step five until you have a good stitch weld in one area, then move to another area of the seam and start over at step one again.

7. With this process, you should be able to weld a 10-inch-long seam in .040-inch aluminum sheet in 5 to 10 minutes.

Another trick of aluminum welding is to lay the torch flame nearly parallel to the surface of the seam if you tend to melt holes in the seam. You may also find that you can melt a couple of drops of weld rod off and onto the seam, then use the torch to flow the drops in to the fusion of the seam.

Tack and Stitch Weld

It is very important to tack-weld several spots along the seam of any thin metal part to control warpage, and this is especially true with welding thin aluminum. And even after you tack-weld several places along the seam, you should stitch weld

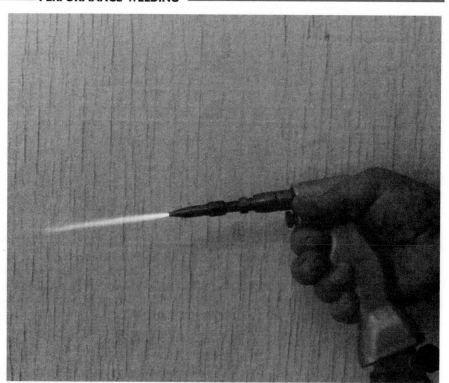

The Dillon/Henrob torch produces a pencil-tip flame rather than a feather-shaped flame common to most gas-welding torches.

A dirty tip on the Dillon/Henrob torch causes a misshapen flame. Note the welding table torch holder that provides a safe place to hang a lighted torch while repositioning the parts to be welded. Never just lay a lighted torch down. That could catch your shop on fire!

short welds of about 1/2-inch long, skipping 1/2-inch, then stitch weld again. Then after you have stitch-welded the entire seam, hammer form the inevitable warped places back into shape, and then weld fill in the gaps between the stitches. Once you get the hang of it, gas welding aluminum will be just another kind of welding. But be sure to wash and wire brush all the flux off the weld seam to prevent future corrosion caused by the flux.

Flange Welding

Where the design of the part will allow it, such as in gas tanks, water tanks, and air duct work, try to incorporate a 90-degree bent-up flange at the weld bead. The flange height should be about double the thickness of the sheet aluminum. If you are welding .040-inch aluminum, the flange should be about .080-inch high. The trick is to butt the two flanges together and just melt them together until they are almost level with the base metal.

You will find that aluminum water tanks and fuel tanks are easy to weld if you provide this melt-down flange for all the welded seams. The reason that it works so well is that the heat of the torch is only concentrated on the edge of the flange and away from the base metal. You will not tend to burn holes if you try to flange weld most thin aluminum assemblies.

Aluminum Brazing

With the advent of new metallurgy and new aluminum alloy combinations, it is becoming easier and easier to produce good, high-strength braze connections in aluminum and magnesium. So try a few samples of aluminum braze materials and test the samples to destruction to see if this process will work for your projects. Chapter 12 gives examples of brazing rod and compatible materials plus strengths of the materials.

Other Uses

For a number of years, oven furnace brazing of aluminum radiators, aluminum air conditioner evaporator cores, and other products have become very common because of the relative simplicity of applying brazing flux and metal powder to an assembly, heating the assembly to slightly above the brazing alloy melting point, but below the aluminum alloy melting point.

A notable use of aluminum brazing is the research and development practice of quickly cutting .100-inch-thick aluminum sheet into computer-drawn patterns that are then stacked and furnace-brazed into one solid piece, producing experimental auto engine blocks and cylinder heads. These experimental parts can be designed and fabricated in a matter of a few days compared to weeks or months for full, solid castings. Aluminum brazing opens up lots of possibilities for research and one-off projects.

All kinds of arc welding—MIG, TIG, stick, and plasma—are sources of ultraviolet radiation. This radiation will burn your skin and especially your eyes. Therefore, cover yourself completely as I have done here. *Gayle Finch*

CHAPTER ELEVEN

SAFETY

I once told my brothers that if any of the three of us die from unnatural causes, it would be from lung problems caused by breathing welding and cutting fumes that we breathed before we learned to protect ourselves from those toxic fumes. In the early days of welding and soldering, unfortunate workers melted and flowed lead all day long, every work day, and obviously inhaled lots of lead before they retired.

Now we know better than to breathe or otherwise expose ourselves to lead, but we still get bit-by-bit inhalings of other toxic fumes that come off of our welding and metal-heating processes. Breathing welding fumes is a long-term danger, but other things are more near-term. Let's take a look at some of the immediate dangers.

Burns

Welding generates high heat, as much as 50,000 degrees F for plasma cutting, and at least 2,700 degrees F for simple fusion welding of steel. One of the most likely welding shop accidents would be to weld one part of a tubular structure and then immediately lean your arm on the extremely hot spot while you are bracing your arm to weld another tube nearby. The hot tube could still be as much as 1,500 degrees F down to 400 degrees F. That would be a cause for a severe burn if you lean your bare arm on the hot tube.

There are several solutions to the accidental burn problem. Wear long leather sleeves and leather gloves while welding tubular structures. Hang temporary tags on each just-

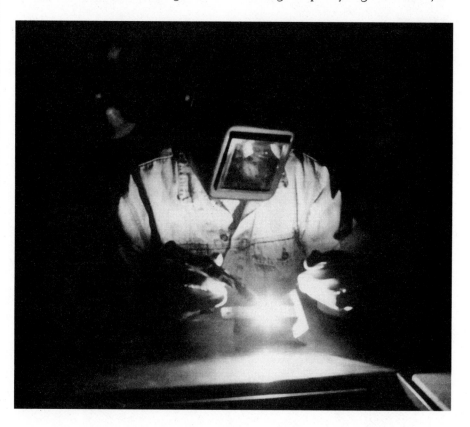

Special breathing hoods are necessary when you are making lots of smoke and sparks from flux-core MIG welding. This welder is properly protected while SAW stick welding. *Sellstrom Manufacturing Company*

welded joint that reads "HOT." And take more time to be sure which parts of the structure are still too hot to touch.

Explosions

A very real and possible danger when welding race car and airplane parts is the danger of welding things that once contained flammable and explosive liquids. I refuse to weld or apply heat or flame to any oil cooler, oil tank, fuel tank, or fuel line unless I know for sure that the item has been completely flushed and purged with an inert gas.

Washing out an oil cooler with cleaning solvent will not make it explosion-proof. Most oil tanks and fuel tanks should be completely boiled out in a caustic type cleaning tank. Steam cleaning is not even a positive way to make a fuel tank or oil cooler safe to weld on. Sometimes it is best to be a coward and refuse to weld any tank, line or radiator that has ever contained a flammable substance. And believe it or not, it is true that 50/50 mixes of ethylene glycol antifreeze are highly flammable and explosive under the right conditions.

So, under what circumstances would I ever weld a used oil radiator or even a used air conditioning evaporator that once had compressor oil in it? I would want to know for sure that it had been boiled out in caustic radiator cleaner. Then I would purge the tank or evaporator with an inert gas, such as argon, before and during the time I am welding it. I surely don't want to take a chance of a tank exploding in my face while I am welding it.

Eye Flash

Another weld shop danger that can cause almost immediate pain is the eye flash from UV rays produced by arc welding. Any electric arc produces ultraviolet rays similar to sunburn. This is a problem that is slow and serious. The first two or three times you get an eye flash from the welding arc, nothing happens. But after one to twelve hours, your eyes will begin to feel like somebody poured sand in them. The only way to ease the pain is usually a trip to a hospital emergency room to get some pain killer for your eyes.

After several welding eye burns, you will be in danger of eye cancer, or at least eye cataracts. You surely don't want that, so protect your eyes and your bystanders' eyes from this serious problem. One overlooked but serious problem with eye flash is your pets—cats, dogs, or any animal that may be fascinated by the bright light of the arc weld.

It is the welder's sole responsibility to shield his weld so that innocent beings, animals or people, cannot accidentally see the UV flash. I keep a small, foldable aluminum shield at my welding table so that I can always shield my arc welds. A secondary benefit of this portable shield is that it also shields my welds from air drafts that could harm them.

Welder's Clothing

It is not necessary to buy or wear the traditional full-leather welding suit and leather apron for making aircraft and race car quality welds. In fact, a heavy, cumbersome full leather jacket would detract from your freedom of movement, even while making MIG welds.

The opposite side of the clothing picture are the many race car welders who like to wear jeans and a racing T-shirt at all times, even while welding. Those guys are sure to get UV burns on their exposed skin, and will also likely burn their arms and their hands just from touching hot metal.

The most convenient welding outfit for a performance welding shop is a good pair of blue jeans, a long-sleeved denim shirt with button-up collar, and a pair of leather lace-up shoes and good cotton socks. If the weather dictates that you must wear a T-shirt in the shop to be comfortable, at least have a denim jacket to wear when you weld, or a button-up long-sleeved shirt to put on over your T-shirt just while you weld.

A good welder should have several different pairs of gloves. I have one pair of dirty, greasy leather gloves that I use when handling new tubing that has dirt and oil all over it. I also keep a couple of pairs of cotton gloves handy for hand protection while I am operating tools and shop equipment such as the band saw, the drill press, the hydraulic press, and the mill. I also keep one new clean pair of canvas gloves for gas welding. Then I have a prized pair of very soft, light gauntlet gloves that are specially made for heliarc welding. Never touch welding rod with dirty, greasy, oil-soaked gloves! And never weld with wet gloves. Oil, grease, dirt, and moisture of the dirty gloves *will* contaminate your welds.

Welding Helmets

Welding helmets come in as many styles and shapes and weights as dress shoes do. There must be hundreds of helmet styles to choose from. For many years I preferred the lightest helmet I could find until a helmet manufacturer pointed out to me that my prized helmet was so small that it did not fully protect my neck while I was welding. So I obtained a larger, longer helmet with a big-window lens, and now it is my prized helmet. Here are some things to look for in shopping for welding helmets:

- Lighter is better—A heavy helmet will tire you faster.
- Rugged construction—A flimsy helmet and headband is bad.
- Style—Buy a helmet for looks, too. This is important.
- Convenience—Try an auto-darkening electronic lens helmet. You may want one.

If you buy a lousy, cheap helmet, you will never be happy with it. Invest a little more for a really nice helmet. Your welds will be better off.

Gas Welding Goggles

Recent developments in gas welding safety goggles have really improved the comfort and convenience factor of wearing eye protection while gas welding and brazing.

Two or three companies presently sell a gas welding goggle that appears to be a $200 pair of ski goggles, but in reality they are high-quality welding goggles that sell for under $10. One

Cotton gloves work just fine for light-duty gas welding and brazing. For TIG welding, wear thin, flexible leather gloves for UV protection. Shield your welds against wind and arc exposure with a solid aluminum shield.

This tub of clear water provides a tank to cool hot parts and it also doubles as an emergency fire extinguisher source.

manufacturer makes a gas welding goggle that fits on your face like a nice pair of sunglasses. And they fit your face tightly so that sparks cannot get inside. Check these goggles out before you settle on the old style pictured in this chapter.

If you wear prescription eye glasses, you must also wear a prescription goggle for welding. Ask your eye care store to show you special lenses for welders. If you can't read this page without prescription glasses, then you can't expect to weld without prescription lenses.

Shop Safety

Many places in this book tell you to clean your parts and your welding rod with acetone, which is almost as flammable as lighter fluid or possibly even gasoline. The procedure for doing this seemingly dangerous practice is to either clean your parts and your welding rod outside the weld area, or clean the parts, then remove the acetone from the weld area before you start welding. You will have to remind yourself often to keep *all* flammables out of the weld shop when you are welding.

Fire Extinguishers

I have a 2 1/2-pound dry chemical fire extinguisher mounted on my welding table, one on my gas welding cart, one on my workbench wall, and one by the door to my shop. I also have a garden-type water hose coiled and ready to use just 4 feet outside the double door to the weld shop. These precautions are cheap fire insurance, and if they are never needed, great. But they are also good peace of mind. Your shop should be similarly equipped.

One negative thing about 2 1/2-pound dry chemical ABC fire extinguishers: They really make a white powdery mess when you use them. So if your budget will allow, buy Halon 1301 or CO_2 fire extinguishers for your shop to avoid the mess caused by the dry powder ones.

General Safety Rules

• Never depend on sight or smell to determine if a container with unknown contents is safe to weld. If in the slightest doubt, clean the cylinder.

• A rather shaky substitute for purging containers, tanks, coolers, and radiators for welding is to fill the item with water to just below where the repair weld is to be made. It can be done this way, but purging is safer.

• Never carry a full or empty acetylene bottle in the closed trunk of a car or inside a van or station wagon. Leaking acetylene fumes can explode with enough force to completely destroy a car, van, or station wagon. Always carry acetylene and flammable gas bottles in an open trailer, open truck, or open pickup bed.

• Hollow castings, containers, or closed tubes must be vented while welding on them to prevent them from exploding from the heat expansion from welding.

• Never weld, cut, or grind where the air may contain flammable dust, gas vapors, natural gas vapors, or flammable liquid vapors.

• If there is *any* possibility of fire danger, such as making a weld repair directly on a vehicle or airplane, have a fire watch person stand by while you are welding.

• If you have a single doubt about the fire or explosive safety of a weld project, just don't do it! Figure out a way to remove the reason for the single doubt.

• Drafts in weld areas are detrimental to the welds, but you should provide for a fume suction system when you are welding things that produce smoke and fumes. Sometimes a fan pointed outside in an open window will remove smoke and fumes sufficiently.

Skin Cancer

Any exposed skin, especially the throat area of the welder, just below the neck, is susceptible to melanoma, or skin cancer, when it is repeatedly exposed to arc welding UV rays. So, always cover everything on your body when MIG, TIG, or arc welding.

MC-Grade welding wire. This desiccant-packaged, 6-pound bag of vacuum melt, metallurgically controlled welding wire from the United States Welding Corporation is by far the best kind of welding rod to use for TIG welds on aircraft and race car projects.

CHAPTER TWELVE

WELDING SUPPLIES, RODS, WIRES, FLUXES

Welding rod comes in grades, just like nuts and bolts do. That's right, you can buy cheap-quality welding rod or you can buy high-quality, certified welding rod. You ask, "What's the difference?"

Here is an example: Airplane builders typically spend $100,000 to build a fast, high-tech airplane. Then they spend $75,000 to purchase a new aircraft engine and propeller for that airplane. Then I ask, does it make economical sense to spend less than $5.00 for the welding rod that holds their engine mount together?

It is a fact that you can go to your local welding supply store and buy 1 pound of no-name copper-coated steel welding rod for as little as $1.50. The welding supply store has no idea what the rod is made out of, except that a magnet will stick to it, so it must be steel, not solid copper, aluminum, or stainless steel. It is also a fact is that the cheap copper-coated steel welding rod is usually made from scrap metal, old cars, old bicycles frames, old tractor parts, and likely a lot of old

concrete reinforcing bars that have been salvaged for scrap value. Not the kind of metal I want to hold my airplane engine mount together with, or to hold the front suspension together on a 250-mile per hour Indy race car.

Until I found a couple of sources for high-quality welding rod, I contacted a large number of local welding supply stores asking for high-quality bare TIG welding rod, *not copper-coated*. Some of the stores I contacted tried to convince me that nobody made such a welding rod. Others said that the quality of the welding rod did not matter, and a couple of the retailers even became angry that I wanted a better welding rod than they had for sale.

Finally I found a manufacturer who sold nothing but high-quality, metallurgically controlled, vacuum-melted, rolled welding rod, and they furnished certification papers with each lot of welding rod they sold. That's my kind of company. Yes, their price for 5 pounds of TIG welding rod was 30 times more expensive than

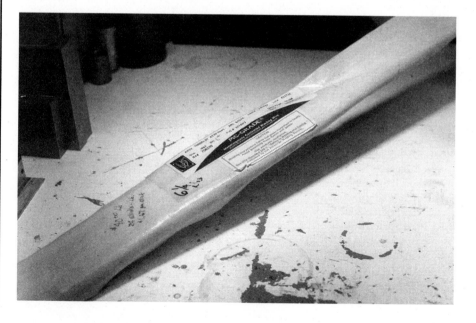

for 5 pounds of the cheap stuff. Even so, I would only have to spend $40 for 1 pound of 4130 steel welding rod to weld the engine mount that holds my $75,000 engine in my $100,000 airplane! Actually, I don't really have an airplane engine or an airplane that costs that much, but a lot of other airplane owners do.

But even if I want to weld an engine mount to hold a $2,000 engine in a $10,000 airplane, $40 for the welding rod versus $1.50 for the cheap rod is not a high price to pay. My own safety and well-being is surely worth the few dollars extra that is charged for the good welding rod.

Nuts and Bolts

At the beginning of this chapter, I equated the grades of welding rod to the various grades of nuts and bolts. You are probably aware of the no-markings bolts that you can buy at the hardware store. These bolts are made from steel of unknown origin, and they can twist in two very easily, so you don't want to use them for anything but lawn furniture. Next comes the grade bolt, called SAE Grade 5, that is commonly used to hold the bumpers and fenders on cars. Next comes the higher-quality bolt that is commonly used to bolt the cylinder head on the car engine. It has 6 marks on the head and it is called SAE Grade 8. And approximately equal in strength to the SAE Grade 8 bolts are the AN bolts, specified for use in missiles and in certified aircraft.

Obviously, the low-grade hardware store bolts should be cheaper than the Grade 8 and AN bolts. And obviously, like in welding rod grades, you don't want to use the cheap stuff in life-support systems such as aircraft and race car assembly.

Results with Cheap Rod

If cheap, reclaimed scrap welding rod is used to TIG or MIG weld 4130 steel, you can expect a number of defects in your welds. Cheap welding rod will bubble and boil and leave big holes in your welds because the cheap stuff has unknown foreign matter in it, including large amounts of dirt, slag, grease, and moisture.

The copper coating on cheap rod does not mix with steel, and it enters the weld puddle to cause defects such

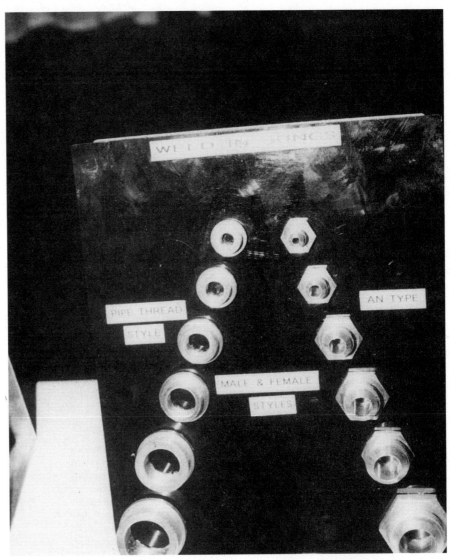

Weld-on fittings like the assortment shown here make an easy job of finishing aluminum oil tanks, fuel tanks, and water recovery tanks. Buy an assortment of these fittings to have on hand for special welding projects.

as crater cracking and hydrogen embrittlement from exposure to moisture trapped between the flaking copper and the cracks and crevices in the cheap rod.

Copper-Coated Rod

In many places in the text of this book, you are advised to use copper as a tungsten arc-starting block, and to use copper strips as back-up strips when welding thin sheets of steel, aluminum, and stainless steel.

We use copper because it will not mix or fuse with steel or other metals. When we use it for a heat-sink back-up strip, we don't have to worry about the copper sticking to our welded seam. When we use copper as an arc-

starting block, we don't have to worry about the nice sharp, pointed tip of our tungsten electrode trying to stick to the copper.

If you cut a cross-section out of a common piece of copper-coated steel welding rod, and magnify it 3,000 times, you will be able to see that the copper coating is not adhering to the rod, but flaking off; the copper coating is not actually a part of the rod.

It will be an obvious question, then, to ask why manufacturers use copper to coat steel welding rod. Copper-coated steel rod will rust, so that is not why they put copper on it. The reason for copper on welding rod is to help make the wire drawing/sizing dies last longer while they are

Bare TIG Rod for 4130 and 4140 Steel

*	USW Stock #6457V	Turbaloy 4130	for 4130 Steel
*	USW Stock #6452V	Turbaloy 4140	for 4140 Steel
**	LAC Stock #6457	AMS 6457	for 4130 Steel
***	A.S. Stock #4130T	æ	for 4130 Steel

Bare TIG Rod for Aluminum and Magnesium

*	USW Stock #4190C	5.2Si	for 6061 and 5052 Aluminum
*	USW Stock #4181C	7 Si	for 356 Castings
*	USW Stock #1374C	5 Mg	for 5052 Aluminum
**	LAC Stock #4190	4043	for 6061 and 5052 Aluminum
**	LAC Stock #4246	AMS357	for 357 Castings
***	A.S. Stock #4043	æ	for 6061 and 5052 Aluminum

Bare TIG Rod for Stainless Steel

*	USW Stock #	AWS A5.9	for 308 Stainless
*	USW Stock #	AWS A5.9	for 316 Stainless
**	LAC Stock #S109	AWS A5.9	for 308 Stainless
**	LAC Stock #5692	AWS A5.9	for 316 Stainless

Bare TIG Rod for Titanium

*	USW Stock #4914C	Alloy 15-3-3-3	Titanium
*	USW Stock #4951C	Alloy C.P.	Titanium
*	USW Stock #4952C	Alloy 6-2-4-2	Titanium
*	USW Stock #4954C	Alloy 6-4	Titanium
*	USW Stock #4955C	Alloy 8-1-1	Titanium
*	USW Stock #4956C	Alloy 6-4 ELI	Titanium
*	LAC Stock #4951	Alloy CP-Ti	Titanium
**	LAC Stock #4954	Alloy 6-4	AWS A5-16
**	LAC Stock #4956	Alloy 6-4 ELI	AWS A5.16(4)

Bare TIG Rod for Magnesium

*	USW Stock #4350C	Alloy AZ61A	Magnesium
*	USW Stock #4395C	Alloy AZ92A	Magnesium
*	USW Stock #4396C	Alloy EZ33A	Magnesium
*	USW Stock #1308C	Alloy AZ101A	Magnesium
*	LAC Stock #4350	Alloy AZ61A	Magnesium
*	LAC Stock #4395	Alloy AZ92A	Magnesium
*	LAC Stock #4396	Alloy AZ33A	Magnesium
**	LAC Stock #M107	Alloy AZ101A	Magnesium

* United States Welding Corporation, Nevada
** Lancaster Alloys Company, California
*** ESAB All-State Welding Products, Maryland

Note: As the advantages of MC grade, vacuum-melt welding rod become better understood by welders, more new and old manufacturers will offer this superb welding material for sale. Meanwhile, do not settle for cheap welding rod for your expensive projects.

Tungsten Electrodes for TIG Welding

Name	Safety Concern	Use For
Pure Tungsten	Nonradioactive	Aluminum
2% Thoriated	Radioactive*	Steel, Stainless Steel
2% Ceriated	Nonradioactive	Orbital Welds
2% Lanthanated	Nonradioactive	Production
Tri-Mix Tungsten	Nonradioactive**	Steel, Stainless Steel

* Thoriated tungsten is radioactive. Extended exposure to radiation can cause cancer.
** Rare-earth mixtures do not contain radiation, yet offer better starting, less degradation, are cooler running, and misfire less on starting.

Note: Two percent Lanthanated tungsten is a rare-earth tungsten, is not radioactive, and offers benefits of improved arc starting, increased electrode life, and higher amperage-carrying capacity.
Two percent Ceriated tungsten is another nonradioactive rare-earth tungsten that is well-suited to automatic orbital pipe and tubing welding.

making the welding rod and wire. The manufacturers also use soaps and oils, which become imbedded in the wire as it is drawn through the dies to size it. Copper is used to lubricate the drawing dies.

M.C. Grade Wire

The metallurgically controlled (MC) welding rod and wire is made from new material that has all its elements traceable and certified. It is melted in vacuum chamber furnaces to prevent atmospheric contamination. Then it is drawn and sized through rollers that squeeze it down to the various sizes it comes in. During each drawing through rollers, it is mechanically wiped clean with acetone or denatured alcohol. No oils, soaps, or greases are used to lubricate the rollers. Only water is used to lubricate the sizing rollers.

At the final sizing for each batch, white-glove inspections are performed and additional cleaning takes place before the rod is vacuum-packaged for shipment to customers. Now you can see where the extra costs come from. And the real proof of quality comes in the welding. MC grade welding rod makes a good welder out of a relatively inexperienced welder. Cheap rod makes it hard for even well-trained welders to handle. For those welders who still have cracks and porosity in your TIG and MIG welds, try some of the good stuff and see how fast you can become a great welder!

Expensive Commercial Grades

There are several welding supply corporations that furnish some really good welding rods and supplies. Notice that I did not say manufacturers. These companies pay other companies to

Tips for TIG Welding

Check out the information in the Gas Welding section of this chapter that refers to fluxes. One particular company that supplies gas welding flux also recommends applying a thick paste mixture of its flux powder and alcohol to the back side of TIG welds on aluminum and stainless steel for vastly improved welds. Check out the Solar Flux data.

make welding rod and supplies to repackage the product under their individual names. Except for the MSD sheets that are required by OSHA, they do not tell the customer what metals and materials are in their products. This practice is common in the welding supply industry. If you ask for certification sheets and can't get them, it is often because another manufacturer makes the supplies, and the second company repackages the product.

However, the fact that you pay $200 for 5 pounds of welding rod does not guarantee a better product. For instance, one particular repackaging company sells a little wire tip

cleaner for gas torches for $45 but a local welding supply store sells the *same* wire tip cleaner for $4.50! It pays to shop for price *and* quality.

Recommended Supplies

The remainder of this chapter is divided into sections that give recommended welding supplies for TIG welding, MIG welding, and gas welding. Finally, there is a section on general welding supplies.

Welding Supplies
Welding Gases

At this time, there are several different methods of obtaining com-

pressed gases for welding. Each geographical location may be unique in how the suppliers allow you to buy consumable gases.

One welding gas retail dealer may lease only. This means that you pay a deposit, $125 for instance, on each gas bottle, then you pay a monthly lease fee, $10 for example, as long as you keep the bottle. And you also pay for the argon gas in the bottle, around $25. In one year, this dealer will get $270 from you for each bottle of gas you lease from him.

Then, just across town, another welding gas retailer may sell you the same size bottle for $125, give you the

MIG Welding Wire Suggestions
Suggested Wire for MIG Welding 4130 and 4140 Steel

	LEC Stock #L-50	AWS A5.18	for 4130 Steel
	LEC Stock# L-50B	AWS A5.18	for 4140 Steel
*	USW Stock #6457V	AWS A5.18	for 4130 Steel
*	USW Stock #6452V	AWS A5.18	for 4140 Steel
**	LAC Stock #6457	AWS A5.18	for 4130 Steel

LEC is Lincoln Electric Company, Ohio

Suggested Wire for MIG Welding Stainless Steel

*	USW Stock #	AWS A5.9	for 308 Stainless
*	USW Stock #	AWS A5.9	for 316 Stainless
**	LAC Stock #3109	AWS A5.9	for 308 Stainless
**	LAC Stock #5692	AWS A5.9	for 316 Stainless

* United States Welding Corporation, Nevada
** Lancaster Alloys Company, California

Do or Don't: Flux and 4130 Steel?

Gas welding (OFW), oxygen-acetylene welding of 4130 steel, does not require any flux, and in fact attempting to use flux on the top side of the weld will make welding very difficult. However, it will aid the welding if a Solar Flux paste is applied to the back side of the weld to aid in heat control on thin sheet-metal butt welds. One difficulty in using flux on 4130 is the requirement that it be removed completely before welding the back side. For the average 4130 tubular structure, no flux should be used.

The Future of Copper-Coated MIG Wire

Welding wire supply companies will eventually offer MIG wire in bare—not copper-coated—rolls. As the welding industry becomes more familiar with the problems caused by copper-coated MIG wire flaking off in the MIG gun and in the cable liner, copper-coated wire will be the exception rather than the rule. Bare wire can rust if not kept covered when not in use. The ideal storage for bare MIG wire is a sealed plastic or metal canister with desiccant inside to prevent moisture from affecting the MIG wire. Copper fumes are unhealthy and copper causes cracking in hot welds. Avoid copper-coated MIG wire on expensive welding projects.

MIG Wire Continues to Change

MIG wire is usually the same chemical mix of alloys as is used in TIG welding the same application. One current problem with MIG wire selection is that every significant company in the business is continuing to experiment with metallurgy to improve weldability of MIG wires. It would be wise to talk to a factory representative about your specific MIG welding requirements before investing in significant amounts of MIG welding wire.

General-Purpose Solder

Cronatron #53 is a very low-temperature solder that melts at only 360 degrees F. And it will join all metals, aluminum to steel, copper, brass, stainless steel, etc., with a 17,500 psi tensile strength. This would be handy in unusual metal-joining situations. It requires a honey-consistency flux to work.

Suggested Welding Rod for Oxyacetylene Steel

*	Oxweld Stock #32CMS	for 4130 Steel
*	USW Stock #6457V	for 4130 Steel
**	A-S Stock #RG-60	for 4130 Steel

* United States Welding Corporation, Nevada
** All-State, ESAB, Maryland

Suggested Weld Rod for Gas Welding Aluminum

1.	CWS Stock #CW1016**	35,000 psi	for 6061 Aluminum
1.	CWS Stock #CW1857**	34,500 psi	for 5052 Aluminum
2.	Welco Stock #COR-AL**	30,000 psi	for 5052 Aluminum
3.	USW Stock #1374C	5 Mg	for 5052 Aluminum

1. CRW is Cronatron Welding Systems, North Carolina
2. Welco is Thermacote - Welco Corporation, Michigan
3. USW is United States Welding Corporation, Nevada

** These aluminum rods are brazing rods, but the 30,000 to 35,000 psi tensile strength should be adequate for most fusion welding of aluminum.

Suggested Weld Rod for Gas Welding Stainless Steel

USW Stock #CW1023	#95 Bare 95,000	TIG or Gas

CWS is Cronatron Welding Systems, North Carolina

Suggested Brazing Rods for Gas Brazing Mild Steel, S.S.

CWS Stock #CW1002 #23F	Blue Coating	66,000	1,400–1,600°F
CWS Stock #CW1836 #30F	Pink Coating	100,000	1,300–1,600°F
CWS Stock #CW1025 #40F	Org (High Silver)	85,000	1,100°F
CWS Stock #CW1024 #43F	Blue Coating	88,000	1,100°F
CWS Stock #CW1017 #53	No Coat (All)	17,500	360°F

CWS is Cronatron Welding Systems, North Carolina

Notes:
23F and 30F are for most regular steel and light cast iron brazing (economical).
40F is a high-priced but excellent high-silver-content silver brazing material that is excellent for stainless steel.
43F is a good, lower-cost silver content brazing rod for steel, copper, brass, and stainless steel.

High-Pressure Cylinder Sizes for Oxygen, Argon, and Helium

Cubic Ft.	OD	Height	Weight	Service Pressure
20	5.27"	14"	10 lb	2015 psi
40	7.0"	18"	23 lb	2015 psi
55	7.0"	23"	30 lb	2015 psi
80	7.0"	33"	42 lb	2015 psi
110	7.0"	43"	55 lb	2015 psi
125	7.0"	43"	55 lb	2265 psi
150	7.0"	46"	59 lb	2015 psi
220	9.0"	51"	114 lb	2015 psi
250	9.0"	51"	115 lb	2265 psi
300	9.27"	55"	135 lb	2400 psi
400	10.50"	66"	190 lb	2400 psi

Low-Pressure Cylinder Sizes for Acetylene

Number	Cubic Ft.	OD	Height	Weight	Service Pressure
S-10	10	4.0"	13"	7.5 lb	250 psi
S-40	40	6.0"	19"	23.4 lb	250 psi
S-75	75	7.0"	26"	43.8 lb	250 psi
S-145	145	8.0"	34"	74.1 lb	250 psi
W210	210	10.0"	32"	100.7 lb	250 psi

Flux-Core Aluminum Brazing Rod

Flux core aluminum brazing rod is relatively new to the gas welding field. When you use it to braze an oil tank made of 5052 aluminum, it is so close to the base metal tensile strength of 36,000 to 41,000 psi that it will give you welds as strong as fusion-welded aluminum. Actually, the lowest tensile strength of 5052-O (soft) aluminum is only 29,000 psi. All of the flux-cored aluminum brazing rod listed in the previous table are above 30,000 psi tensile strength. The melting point of these flux-cored brazing rods is 1,050 degrees F to 1,100 degrees F, just over 100 degrees F lower than the 1,217 degrees F melting point of the base metal, a difference that is not really controllable with a hand-operated oxyacetylene torch. Generally, you will end up with a good fused weld/braze joint anyway.

As in gas welding stainless steel, try to make each seam a 90-degree folded joint so that most of the heat is applied to the fold and not the flat base metal.

first fill of argon free, and of course you don't have to pay him a monthly rent on the bottle, because you bought it. You can keep the bottle for a year and sell it to a friend or back to the dealer. So you saved $145 the first year on each bottle you bought rather than leased. This exact situation exists in the town where I live. So as this book tells you over and over, shop around before you buy!

Bottle Sizes

Don't make the mistake of buying or leasing the largest gas bottles or the smallest gas bottles, even if you are operating a full-time welding fabrication shop. The largest bottles will be a nuisance to handle, and the smallest ones go empty far too quickly. The charts in this chapter will help you decide the right size cylinders for your shop.

Fluxes

In researching 10 flux supplier catalogs, it becomes obvious that no company will tell the consumer what chemicals they put in their products to make them do the special protecting and cleaning jobs that each brand is advertised to do. And if you attempted to buy one of every part number, you would really be confused, because 10 manufacturers make over 100 different products. Below are listed a few of the better or best fluxes with descriptions of how each one works.

Solar Flux (formerly Solar Aircraft, San Diego, CA)
Golden Empire Corporation
P.O. Box 2129
Morehead City, NC 28557
Phone: (919) 808-3511

Superior Flux and Manufacturing Company
95 Alpha Park
Cleveland, OH 44143
Phone: (216) 461-3315

Bradford Derustit Corporation
P.O. Box 151
Clifton Park, NY 12065
Phone: (201) 485-7922

For special jobs, contact the manufacturer or your local welding supply retailer to find specific fluxes for specific metals and preferred joining methods.

Names and Addresses of Welding Supply Companies Listed in this Chapter

Aircraft Spruce and Specialty Company
201 W. Truslow Avenue
P.O. Box 424
Fullerton, CA 92836
Orders: (800) 824-1930
Product Information: (714) 871-7551
Fax: (714) 871-7289

Cronatron Welding Systems, Inc.
6510 Northpark Boulevard
Charlotte, NC 28216-2367
Phone: (704) 598-1225

ESAB All-State Welding Products
5112 Allendale Lane
P.O. Box 600
Taneytown, MD 21787
Phone: (800) 638-1647
Phone (410) 756-4330

Lancaster Alloys Company
43210 Gingham Avenue, Unit 4
Lancaster, CA 93535
Phone: (800) LA-WIRES
Phone: (805) 723-1397

Recommended Gases for Welding

Welding Process	Suggested Gases
TIG Aluminum	Argon
TIG 4130 Steel	Argon
TIG Stainless Steel	Argon
TIG Titanium	Argon
MIG Aluminum	Argon
MIG 4130 Steel	75%–25% Argon and Helium
MIG Stainless Steel	Argon + 1% Oxygen
OFW Aluminum	Oxygen and Acetylene or Hydrogen
OFW 4130 Steel	Oxygen and Acetylene
OFW Stainless Steel	Oxygen and Acetylene
Inert Gas Purging	Argon

Be sure to ask your welding gas supply dealer to explain his special gas mixture to aid your MIG welding needs. Certain companies offer "Gold Mix," which is 70 percent argon, 12 percent helium, and 18 percent special mix, or other unusual percentages. Their experience tells them that even as little as 1 percent oxygen can greatly improve certain welding processes.

Mil-Spec Fluxes

Solar Flux 1-pound Containers	Type 1	For nickel, Inconel, etc. Mix with methanol to form a thick paste. Works well to clean and to protect the back side of gas, TIG, and MIG welds.
Solar Flux 1-pound Containers	Type B	For all stainless steels. Mix with methanol to form a thick paste. Apply to back side of gas, MIG, and TIG welds to assure sugar-free welds.
Solar Flux 1-pound Containers	Type 202	For all gas welds on aluminum. Works well with TIG or MIG also. Makes gas welding aluminum easy to do.

Number 65 Flux

No. 65	Flux for welding and soldering all metals except aluminum and magnesium. For air conditioners, refrigeration, stainless. 200–600 degrees F.

Metal Cleaners

Derustit SS-3	Stainless steel cleaner. Cleans heat scale off stainless steel welds.
Bradford No. 1	Metal cleaner. Cleans steel, copper, brass. Rust oxide remover.

Backup Pastes for Weld Protection and Jigging

HTP Stock #12084 Heat Sponge, Ceramic Heat Sink
CWS Stock #CW1082A Plio Jig, Ceramic Heat Sink
Check with your local welding supply retailer for 1- and 5-pound plastic cans of a moist, clay-like ceramic paste that will insulate your welds. These products work like putting a water-soaked rag by the weld to insulate the heat from the parts you don't want to overheat

United States Welding Corporation
3579 Highway 50 East #104
Carson City, NV 89701-2826
Phone: (800) 423-5964
Phone: (702) 883-7878

Thermacote-Welco Company
32311 Stephenson Highway
Madison Heights, MI 48071
Phone: (313) 588-1122

CONTENTS

CHAPTER THIRTEEN

SOURCES FOR METALS

You may already have a favorite place where you buy 4130 steel tubing, 6061 aluminum, and 308 and 316 stainless steel. If you are buying it through a local metals dealer, it would be a good idea to check around to see if you are getting certified materials and to see if you are paying a fair price.

There are metals dealers who claim they are the primary source for most other retail outlets, and that, therefore, they have the biggest selection and the best prices. In this short chapter I am listing several companies who sell retail quantities of aluminum, steel, and various metals that you need to use in your performance welding projects. They are not listed in any specific order of preference, rather they are in an easy-to-read, alphabetic order.

A B C Metals and Supply Company
2931 Ventura Boulevard
Oxnard, CA 93031

Phone: (805) 485-7805
Fax: (805) 981-0394

Aircraft Spruce East
900 S. Pine Hill Road
P.O. Box 901
Griffin, GA 30224
Orders: (800) 831-2949
Product Information: (770) 228-3901
Fax: (770) 229-2329

Aircraft Spruce Europe
8 Cam Center, Wilbury WY
Hitchin, Hertfordshire
England SG4 0TW
Phone: (01) 462-441995
Fax: (01) 462-442228

Aircraft Spruce and Specialty
  Company West
201 W. Truslow Avenue
P.O. Box 424
Fullerton, CA 92836
Orders: (800) 824-1930
Product Information: (714) 871-7551
Fax: (714) 871-7289

Here I am unpacking and inspecting a shipment of 4130 steel tubing that I just received. Within a few days, the tubing was cut, fitted, and welded into an airplane fuselage assembly.

Aircraft Steel (and Aluminum)
923 W.C.R. #7
Erie, CO 80516
Phone: (303) 665-5817

CSC Racing Products Inc.
163 Bowes Rd. #1
Concord, Ontario
Canada L4K1H3
Phone: (905) 738-2238

The Dillsburg Aeroplane Works
114 Saw Mill Road
Dillsburg, PA 17019
Phone: (717) 432-4589

Ducommun Metals and Supply
    Company
4890 S. Alameda Street
Los Angeles, CA 90054
Phone: (213) 588-0161

Industrial Metal Supply Company
3303 N. San Fernando Boulevard
Burbank, CA 91504
Phone: (818) 781-0114
Phone: (818) 848-4439
Phone: (714) 552-3702

Ryerson Steel and Aluminum
780 N. Colony Road
Wallingford, CT 06492
Phone: (203) 269-0772

Ventura Steel, Inc.
1885 N. Ventura Avenue
Ventura, CA 93001
Phone: (805) 643-6662
Phone: (800) 235-0099
Fax: (805) 643-6667

Wag Aero Group
P.O. Box 181
Lyons, WI 53148
Phone: (800) 558-6868

Wicks Aircraft Supply
410 Pine Street
Highland, IL 62249
Phone: (618) 654-7447
Phone: (800) 221-9425
Fax: (618) 654-6253

The companies listed above were valid and the addresses and telephone numbers were correct at the time of publication. Be aware of the fact that many companies merge with other companies and change their names, addresses, and telephone numbers in the process of merging.

If you are unable to contact one of these companies in your area, just look in your current telephone directory under the heading of "Steel Products" or "Metals" for new companies who sell aircraft quality metals.

Shop by Phone

Even if you do not live near one of the metals supply companies listed in this chapter, you can call them and order steel, aluminum, and stainless steel over the telephone. Most metals companies do a lot of their business by shipping orders by truck and by United Parcel Service (UPS). Shipping fees are usually from 2 percent to 5 percent of the total order price.

If the metal tubing you order measures more than 8 feet long, it cannot be shipped by UPS; but most truck lines will deliver it to your door, even in residential areas. Once or twice in many years of ordering tubing, I have encountered truck lines that want the shipment picked up at their dock, but usually the truck drivers are happy to deliver to my shop door.

Catalogs

Every metals supply company listed in this chapter can supply you with a catalog listing the materials they have for sale. In several of the available catalogs, extra information is presented, such as I.D., O.D., strength of materials, common manufacturing practices, and other pertinent information for the buyer. Some of the catalogs are free to any user who calls for one, and other companies sell their catalogs with a coupon that is refundable with the first purchase. Most of the companies who furnish catalogs also include many other useful items in them.

All aircraft and aerospace metals should have factory markings that identify the material, such as on this sheet of 4130 steel.

Material that is left over from airplane or race car projects can be used to build other handy things. I used 3/4-inch square tubing from a previous race car project to build this roll-around cabinet frame for my sandpaper and glass bead cabinet abrasives.

CHAPTER FOURTEEN

SHOP MATH

As it often happens in welding, you find a requirement for knowing a formula to calculate the amount of metal needed to complete a project, or you may need to know how much extra weight will be added to a structure to add a strengthening gusset or brace. The most often-used formulas and charts are included in this chapter. Study the chapter to familiarize yourself with its contents so you will be able to find the information quickly when you need it.

The Metric System

In 1886, the United States government legalized the use of the metric measurement system in America and, as of today, well over 100 years later, we Americans are still hanging onto the inch and pound measurements, and having trouble converting between the two measuring systems. In the following tables, simple equivalents are given to help the welder compare measurements.

Measurement Conversion Tables

Table 1. Measures of Length

1 millimeter (mm)	=	—	=	0.03937 inch
10 millimeters	=	1 centimeter	=	0.393 inch
10 centimeters	=	1 decimeter	=	3.937 inches
10 decimeters	=	1 meter	=	39.37 inches
10 meters	=	1 dekameter	=	32.808 feet
10 hektometers	=	1 kilometer	=	0.621 mile
10 kilometers	=	1 mm	=	6.213 miles

Table 2. Measures of Weight

1 gram	=	15.432 grains	=	0.035 oz.
10 grams	=	1 dekagram	=	0.352 oz.
10 dekagrams	=	1 hektogram	=	3.527 oz.
10 hektograms	=	1 kilogram	=	2.204 lb.
1,000 kilograms	=	1.102 tons	=	2,204.621 lb.

Table 3. Measures of Capacity

1 liter	=	1.056 quarts	=	61.027 cubic inches
10 liters	=	2.641 gallons	=	2.641 gallons
10 dekaliters	=	1 hektaliter	=	2.8375 bushels
10 hektaliters	=	1 kiloliter	=	61,027.05 cubic inches

Table 4. Miscellaneous Measures

1 cubic foot	=	28.317 liters
1 gallon	=	3.785 liters
1 cubic centimeter	=	0.61 cubic inches
100 cubic centimeters	=	6.1027 cubic inches
1,000 cubic centimeters	=	61.027 cubic inches
1 liter	=	61.027 cubic inches

Shop Math Formulas

Area of a Circle

To find the area of a circle, multiply the square of the circle diameter by .7854.

Example:
The diameter of the circle is 12 inches. Multiply 12 x 12 = 144.
Multiply 144 x .7854 = 113.0976.

Answer: The area of the 12-inch diameter circle is 113.0976 square inches.

Circumference of a Circle

To find the circumference of a circle, multiply the diameter by 3.1416 (pi).

Example:
The diameter of the circle is 12 inches. Multiply 12 x 3.1416 = 37.6992.

Answer: The circumference of the 12-inch diameter circle is 37.6992 inches.

Area of Annular Ring

To find the area of an annular ring, calculate the areas of the outer circle and the inner circle, then subtract the inner area from the outer area for the answer.

Example:
12 x 12 inches = 144 x .7854 = 113.0976
8 x 8 inches = 64 x .7854 = 50.2656
113.0976 - 50.2656 = 62.832

Answer: The area of the annular ring is 62.832 square inches.

Area of a Square

To find the area of a square, multiply the length by the width.

Example:
12 x 12 inches = 144 square inches

Area of a Rectangle

To find the area of a rectangle, multiply the length by the width.

Example:
8 x 12 inches = 96 square inches

Area of a Parallelogram

To find the area of a parallelogram, multiply the base by the perpendicular height.

Example:
12 x 8 inches = 96 square inches

Area of a Sphere

To find the area of a sphere, multiply the square of the diameter by 3.1416.

Example:
12 x 12 inches = 144
144 inches x 3.1416 = 452.3904

Answer: The area of the sphere is 452.3904 square inches.

Volume of a Sphere

To find the volume of a sphere (cubic contents), multiply the cube of the diameter by .5236.

Example:
12 x 12 x 12 inches = 1,728
1728 x .5236 = 904.7808

Answer: The volume of the sphere is 904.7808 cubic inches.

Volume of a Cylinder

To find the volume of a cylinder (as in a V-6 or V-8 engine), multiply the area of one end of the cylinder by the length of the cylinder. The product will be the cubic contents of the cylinder. In an engine, measure and calculate the bore by the stroke in inches or millimeters.

Example:
Bore = 4.0 inches; 4 x 4 = 16 x .7854 = 12.5664
Stroke = 4.0 inches; 4 x 12.5664 = 50.2656

Answer: The volume of the cylinder is 50.2656 cubic inches.
V-8 engine = 8 (cylinders) x 50.2656 = 402.1248

Answer: The V-8 engine displaces 402.1248 cubic inches.

Volume of a Cube

To find the volume of a cube, multiply the length by the width by the height. The product will be the cubic inch or cubic centimeter volume of the cube.

Example:
12 x 12 inches = 144 x 12 inches = 1,728

Answer: The volume of the cube is 1,728 cubic inches.

Volume of a Cone

To find the volume of a cone, multiply the square of the base by the perpendicular height and the result by .2618.

Example:
12 x 12 inches = 144 x 12 inches = 1,728
1,728 x .2618 = 452.3904

Answer: The volume of the cone is 452.3904 cubic inches.

Gear Ratios

To calculate a gear ratio, when the number of the input and output gear teeth are known, divide the small number of teeth into the large number of teeth.

Example:
Input teeth = 12
Output teeth = 38
38 ÷ 12 = 3.16667

Answer: The gear ratio is 3.16667:1.

Compound Gear Ratios

To calculate a compound gear ratio where three or more gears are used to slow something down or speed it up, calculate the ratio in steps, because that is actually what is happening in the gear ratio.

Example:
Divide 12 teeth into 24 teeth = 2
Divide 2 into 12 = 6
Divide 6 into 36 = 6

Answer: The gear reduction ratio is 1:6.

Distance Per Revolutions

To calculate the distance a vehicle travels when its drive tire rotates one time, multiply the height (diameter) of the drive tire by 3.1416 (pi).

Example:
The vehicle has a drive tire that is 28 inches tall.
Multiply 28 inches x 3.1416 = 87.9648.

Answer: The vehicle travels 87.9648 inches.

Revolutions Per Distance

To find out how many revolutions a vehicle tire turns in a certain forward (or backward) distance, multiply the height (diameter) of the tire by 3.1416 (pi) and then divide that product into the known distance traveled.

Example:
The vehicle has 28-inch tall tires and it travels 1 mile (5,280 feet, or 63,360 inches)
Multiply 28 inches by 3.1416 = 87.9648 inches
Divide 63,360 inches by 87.9648 inches = 720.28811

Answer: The tires turn 720.3 revolutions per mile.

Properties of Metals—No Specific Alloys

Metal	Wt./Cu. Ft. (pound)	Tensile Strength (psi)	Melting Point (degrees F)
Aluminum	166.5	15,000–64,000	1,140
Brass	523.2	30,000–45,000	1,600
Copper	552.0	30,000–40,000	1,930
Gold, Pure	1,200.9	20,380	2,100
Iron, Cast	450.0	20,000–35,000	2,200
Lead	709.7	1,000–7,000	618
Silver, Pure	655.1	40,000	1,800
Steel	489.6	50,000–280,000	2,400
Tin	458.3	5,000–10,000	475
Zinc	436.5	3,500	780

Decimals Versus Gauge Numbers for Sheet Metal

Aluminum Thickness in Decimals	Steel Thickness in Decimals	Old Gauge Designation
.010-inch	.012-inch	30
.012-inch	.014-inch	29
.016-inch	.016-inch	27
.020-inch	.020-inch	25
.025-inch	.030-inch	22
.032-inch	.035-inch	20
.040-inch	.048-inch	18
.050-inch	.060-inch	16
.065-inch	.075-inch	14
.080-inch	.104-inch	12
.090-inch	.120-inch	11
.100-inch	.135-inch	10
.125-inch	.165-inch	8
.1875-inch	.210-inch	5
.250-inch	1/4-inch	1/4-inch

SAE Bolt Torque Values

Size	Grade 5 In-Lb Ft-Lb	Grade 8 Newton Meters Ft-Lb	In-Lb	Newton Meters
1/4-20	95 in-lb.	11	125 in-lb.	14
1/4-28	95 in-lb.	11	150 in-lb.	17
5/16-18	200 in-lb.	23	270 in-lb.	31
5/16-24	20 ft-lb.	27	25 ft-lb.	34
3/8-16	30 ft-lb.	41	40 ft-lb.	54
3/8-24	35 Fft-lb.	48	45 ft-lb.	61
7/16-14	50 ft-lb.	68	65 ft-lb.	88
7/16-20	55 ft-lb.	75	70 ft-lb.	95
1/2-13	75 ft-lb.	102	100 ft-lb.	136
1/2-20	85 ft-lb.	115	110 ft-lb.	149
9/16-12	105 ft-lb.	142	135 ft-lb.	183
9/16-18	150 ft-lb.	156	150 ft-lb.	203
5/8-11	115 ft-lb.	203	195 ft-lb.	264
5/8-18	160 ft-lb.	217	210 ft-lb.	285
3/4-16	175 ft-lb.	237	225 ft-lb.	305

Circular Measurements
60 seconds = 1 minute
60 minutes = 1 degree
30 degrees = 2 sign
90 degrees = 1 quadrant
4 quadrants = 360 degrees
360 degrees = 1 circle

Sheet Metal Gauges Versus Thousandths-of-an-Inch

Sheet metal designations are slowly changing to utilize current metallurgy and current fabrication processes. For instance, aluminum is now designated as 6061-T6 rather than the old designation of 61S-T. If you were planning to build an engine oil tank, you would specify .050-inch 6061-T4 aluminum sheet rather than the old designation of 18-gauge 61S-W aluminum.

Only the most common thicknesses of sheet metal are listed in the accompanying charts.

Metric Thread and Grade Identification

Metric and inch thread notations differ slightly. Common metric fastener strength property classes are 9.8 and 12.9 with the class identification embossed on the head of each bolt. Inch strength classes range from Grade 2 to Grade 8 with line identification embossed on each bolt head. Markings correspond to two lines less than the actual grade (for example, a Grade 7 bolt will exhibit five embossed lines on the bolt head). Some metric nuts will be marked with single-digit strength identification numbers on the nut face.

AN and MS Torque Chart
Recommended Nut Torques for Aircraft Hardware

The torque values stated in the following charts are in inch-pounds,
related only to oil-free cadmium-plated threads.

Fine Thread Series Nut

Tension	Shear	Std (Note 1)	Alt (Note 2)	Std (Note 3)	Alt8-36	12-15	7-9
10-32	20-25	20-28	12-15	12-19			
1/4-28	50-70	50-75	30-40	30-48			
5/16-24	100-140	100-150	60-85	60-106			
3/8-24	160-190	160-260	95-110	95-170			
7/16-20	450-500	450-560	270-300	270-390			
1/2-20	480-690	480-730	290-410	290-500			
9/16-18	800-1000	800-1070	480-600	480-750			
5/8-18	1100-1300	1100-1600	660-780	660-1060			
3/4-16	2300-2500	2300-3350	1300-1500	1300-2200			
7/8-14	2500-3000	25004650	1500-1800	1500-2900			
1-14	3700-5500	3700-6650	2200-3300	2200-4400			
1-1/8-12	5000-7000	5000-10000	3000-4200	3000-6300			
1-1/4-12	9000-11000	9000-16700	5400-6600	5400-10000			

Coarse Thread Series Nut

Tension	Shear	(Note 4)	(Note 5)
8-32	12-15		7-9
10-24	20-25		12-15
1/4-20	40-50		25-30
5/16-18	80-90		48-55
3/8-16	160-185		95-100
7/16-14	235-255		140-155
1/2-13	400-480		240-290
9/16-12	500-700		300-420
5/8-11	700-900		420-540
3/4-10	1150-1600		700-950
7/8-9	2200-3000		1300-1800
1-8	3700-5000		2200-3000
1/18-8	5500-6500		3300-4000
1/14-8	6500-8000		4000-5000

Notes:
1. Covers AN310, AN315, AN345, AN363, AN366, MS20365, 1452, EB, UWN, Z1200, and other self-locking nuts.
2. When using AN310 or AN320 castellated nuts where alignment between bolt and cotter pin is not reached using
   normal torque values, use alternate torque values or replace nut.
3. Covers An316, AN320, AN7502, and MS20364.
4. Covers AN310, AN340, AN366, MS20365, and other self-locking anchor nuts.
5. Covers AN316, AN320, and MS20364.

Metric Bolt Torque Values

Size	NM Torque	In-Lb. Torque
6	0.4	4
6.3	0.4	4
8	0.8	7
10	1.4	12
12	2.2	18
14	3.0	25
16	4.2	35
20	7.0	57

A GLOSSARY OF TERMS

A

arc strike	An accidental discontinuity of arcing in the base metal out of the weld.
arc welding	Also called stick welding. Proper term is SMAW for "shielded metal arc welding."

B

backfire	The momentary recession of the oxyacetylene flame back into the welding tip followed by immediate reappearance or complete extension of the flame. A dangerous event!
backing plate	Usually a strip of copper that is placed on the back side of the weld to prevent molten metal drop-through and to prevent holes from being melted in thin material.
bare electrode	A piece of filler metal that is intended to be used as the arc source and the filler metal, as in MIG welding.
base metal	The metal that is to be welded, brazed, soldered, cut, or that has been welded.
bead	See weld bead.
blowhole	Another term for porosity.
brazing	The operation where capillary action of silver, brass, or copper adheres to the base metal and at a temperature above 840 degrees F.
burn through	Excessive heat applied to the base metal or an actual hole melted through the weld seam that must be patched before continuing the weld.
butt joint	Where two pieces of metal are joined, end-to-end, with no lap, usually in the same plane.
butt weld	Where a butt joint is welded.

C

capillary action	The force by which a liquid in contact with a solid or another liquid of equal viscosity and temperature is attracted to the other liquid, as in two puddles of water on a solid or two puddles of weld, braze, or solder that are attracted to each other. In other words, in welding, brazing, or soldering, the heated, liquid puddle of metal is attracted to other similar metals and to the heated base metal. It wants to attach itself to something hot.
carburizing flame	As in oxyacetylene welding, a flame that is not adjusted for equal parts of oxygen and acetylene. Too much acetylene and the flame will be soot-producing and will induce cracks in low-alloy steel. Modern gas welding should never be carburizing.
chamfer	To bevel a piece of metal for more weld bead buildup.

cold crack	A crack that develops after welding because the metal was exposed to contamination while welding. Contamination includes things such as dirty base metal, dirty welding rod, insufficient shielding gas, cheap-quality welding rod, or wind blowing on the hot weld.
crater crack	A crack usually caused by stopping the weld at full power without adding additional filler metal. But it also can be caused by dirt, poor shielding gas, or cheap welding rod. A defect in the weld.
cold weld	The lack of penetration of the weld bead caused by too little heat applied to the weld base metal. Usually should be ground out and rewelded.
cone	The conical part of any oxyfuel gas flame next to the orifice of the tip.
consumable	Any item used in welding that is usually consumed during the welding or cutting process, such as the copper orifices that naturally wear away in plasma arc cutting, or the bare welding rod used in TIG or gas welding, or the bare wire used in MIG welding. Can also be the coated electrode used in stick welding.
cored wire	As used in wire-feed welding, the welding filler metal has flux inside the wire for gasless MIG welding, usually a dirty, smoky process.
cutting torch	Usually in oxyacetylene cutting, the special attachment that allows certain metals to be cut by the oxygen process, but it can also be used to describe the plasma arc cutting process that will cut all metals with a high-temperature arc and air pressure.

D

defect	A crack or porosity in a weld that makes the weld weak and ineffective. Also called a flaw in the weld.
depth of fusion	The depth into the base metal that the molten puddle extends, usually specified in percent, such as 15 percent to 100 percent. Also called penetration.
duty cycle	The percentage of 10-minute blocks of time a welding machine can operate without losing power or overheating. If the duty cycle of a specific welding machine is 20 percent at 175 amps, it can weld for 2 minutes, then it must rest and cool for 8 minutes before it can weld again.

E

electrode	A wire used in MIG welding, a covered stick of wire used in arc welding, or a tungsten used in TIG welding that usually indicates that electricity flows through the electrode to produce an arc for welding. Not a description of filler wire used in gas welding or TIG welding.
electrode holder	In stick welding, the clamp that holds the covered welding rod, or in TIG welding, the torch body that holds the tungsten electrode.

F

face shield	A clear plastic or Lexan™ shield used to protect the face and eyes from grinding and blasting particles.
filler rod	Also called filler metal, it is the welding wire that is added to the weld puddle to complete the weld. It is highly important to use good-quality filler rod, not brazing rod, when welding aircraft and race car parts.

filler wire	Usually MIG or wire-feed welding wire, but it can also be TIG or gas welding wire (rod).
fillet weld	A weld bead of triangular cross-section joining two pieces or more of metal at approximately right angles to each other.
fixture	A device used to hold parts in the proper relationship for welding.
flange weld	A weld made on the flanged edges of two or more pieces of thin metal, as in welding a gas tank or water tank.
flashback	A recession of the oxyacetylene flame back into the mixing chamber of the torch. A dangerous event!
flat position	The easiest and most desirable welding position to make welds, as in writing on a desk.
flux	A material, usually powder or liquid, used to prevent, dissolve, or remove oxides from metal to be welded, brazed, or soldered. Usually a chemical.
freezing point	The temperature at which a specific metal goes from liquid to solid.
fuel gas	A flammable gas such as acetylene, natural gas, propane, butane, MAPP gas, and hydrogen. The fuel gas is usually mixed with equal parts of gaseous oxygen for heating.

G

gas cylinder	A portable container used for storing compressed gases, usually at high pressure.
GMAW	Gas Metal Arc Welding, also called MIG welding, Metallic Inert welding, or wire-feed welding.
GTAW	Gas Tungsten Arc Welding, also called TIG welding, Tungsten Inert Gas Welding, and Heliarc™ welding.
gas welding	Also called OFW for OxyFuel Welding, because several different fuel gases can be used, such as hydrogen and propane. Oxyacetylene welding is the most common.
ground connection	An electrical connection that is necessary to complete the circuitry in arc, TIG, and MIG welding. Also called the ground clamp.

H

heat-affected zone	The portion of the base metal that has not been melted, but whose mechanical properties or microstructure has been altered by the welding heat. In steel, the color of the base metal changes to blue to indicate the heat-affected zone.
helmet	The hood worn over the face while arc welding that includes the tinted lens for face and eye protection from ultraviolet rays produced in all arc welding.

I

inert gas	Usually argon, CO_2, or helium used to protect the weld from atmospheric contamination. Inert gas, however, does not clean a dirty weld.
interpass temperature	In a weld that requires more than one weld bead to build up to base metal thickness, the weld must be allowed to cool to a much lower temperature to prevent "burning" the weld by overheating the base metal when making additional weld passes.

J

joint	The meeting point of two or more parts to be welded. Also describes a connection of parts made by welding.
joint type	There are five basic joint types: butt joint, lap joint, corner joint, edge joint, and T-joint.

K

kerf	The width of the gap that is produced when cutting a material.

L

liquidius	The temperature of metal that takes it from solid to molten.
local preheat	A process used to preheat a large structure before welding when the structure will not fit inside an oven.

M

melt	The process where metal is heated to the temperature that converts it from a frozen solid to a liquid.
MIG	See GMAW.

N

neutral flame	An adjustment that allows gas welding to produce a flame that is neither oxidizing (excess oxygen) or carburizing (excess fuel gas).

O

oxidizing flame	In gas welding, a flame that has excess oxygen, as in a cutting torch for cutting steel.
OFW	See gas welding.

P

penetration	In all types of fusion welding, the depth into the base metal that a temperature penetrated to cause the filler rod to fuse the metal together.
plasma	As in plasma arc cutting, plasma arc welding, and other metal-working procedures, this process produces arc temperatures reaching 50,000 degrees F.
plug weld	Also called a rosette weld, a circular hole in the outer tube to fuse weld to an inner tube.
polarity	Direct current (electrode negative) or direct current (electrode positive), as in DC welding.
porosity	Cavity-type defects in welds caused by dirt, copper, or gas entrapment while the weld puddle is molten but freezing.
post flow	The number of seconds that the inert gas is adjusted to flow after the weld is stopped for the purpose of protecting the weld as it cools.
preheat	The process used to raise the temperature of assemblies to be welded so that the heat of welding will not shock or crack the base metal, usually 350 degrees F. It also aids in producing faster weld puddle times.
puddle	When metal melts in the area to be welded, it forms a liquid area which is called the puddle.

R

reducing flame	An excess acetylene or excess fuel flame. Also called a carburizing flame. Avoid it.
reverse polarity	In DC welding, this means that the electrode is positive. It is also called plus (+) polarity, as opposed to straight (−) or negative polarity.

S

shielding gas A protective gas, usually but not always inert, that is used to protect the weld from oxygen, hydrogen, and other atmospheric contamination.

solder A filler metal used to join metals by surface tension and capillary action at temperatures below 840 degrees F.

stick welding Called FCAW, for Flux Covered Arc Welding, or arc welding. A process ordinarily used in building bridges and fabricating farm equipment. Not for building airplanes or race cars.

stitch weld Usually done where 100-percent welds are not required for strength. The welds are usually 1/2-inch to 1-inch long with equal gaps between the welds.

straight polarity As in DC welding, the electrode is negative. Also called reverse polarity or negative polarity, this is the most common setting for TIG welding steel, stainless steel, and titanium.

stress relief The process of slowly heating the welded assembly to a temperature near the melting point, holding it at that temperature for minutes to hours, then slowly cooling the assembly to room temperature. This process cannot be correctly done by manual heat application.

T

tack weld A small weld made to hold parts of a weldment in proper alignment until the final fitting and final welds are made. A very necessary part of the welding process.

temporary weld Usually made to hold parts together for fit checking, where the weld or part will be removed for further fitting or assembly. Similar to a tack weld, but larger and stronger.

TIG welding See GTAW.

U

undercut The bane of beginning welders. A groove melted into the base metal at the edge of the weld bead and left unfilled by the weld filler metal. It can be corrected by running a second weld pass to fill the undercut, and proper heat application can prevent undercut.

V

vacuum melt A process used to make high-quality castings and high-quality welding wire where 99 percent of atmospheric contamination is vacuumed and removed from the melting furnace.

vacuum welds Contamination-free welds that are made in a vacuum chamber. See Chapter 5 for pictures of vacuum chamber welding equipment.

W

weld To melt the base metal so that the puddle joins the puddle from the other piece of base metal, then becomes permanently a part of each other as the molten puddle freezes. A process where the base metal is locally heated to above the melting point.

welder The person who operates the welding equipment to perform welding operations.

welding machine The equipment used to perform the welding operation.

weld position	The position of the material to be welded. The position can be flat, horizontal, vertical, or overhead, but flat is always the best.
welding rod	Usually used to describe flux-coated stick electrode used in arc welding. But the term is also correct to describe the 36-inch-long bare welding rod used in gas welding and TIG welding, but usually when the rod measures over 1/16-inch in diameter. Smaller rod is usually called wire.
welding wire	Usually used to describe MIG welding wire, either flux-cored or solid, that comes on rolls. It can also be used to describe gas or TIG welding filler metal in diameters of less than 1/16-inch (.063 inch).
weld pass	A single progression of the weld bead along a joint. Multiple weld passes (beads) are used in thick materials, such as "I" beams for bridge building or heavy pipe for oil and gas pipelines.
wetting	The phenomenon whereby a liquid metal or flux spreads and sticks in a thin, continuous layer on the base metal. It is usually used to describe brazing and soldering.
weld symbols	The standard symbols used by engineers to properly call out the desired welds in weldable assemblies.

WELDING & FABRICATING ORGANIZATIONS

ANSI
American National Standards Institute
11 W. 42nd Street
New York, NY 10036
(212) 354-3300

API
American Petroleum Institute
1220 L Street N.W.
Washington, DC 20005
(202) 682-8000

ASCE
American Society of Civil Engineers
345 E. 47th Street
New York, NY 10017
(212) 705-7496

ASME
American Society of Mechanical
 Engineers
345 E. 47th Street
New York, NY 10017
(800) 843-2763

ASTM
American Society for Testing and
 Materials
1916 Race Street
Philadelphia, PA 19013
(215) 299-5400

AWS (the primary organization for
 welding)
American Welding Society
550 N.W. Le Jeune Road
Miami, FL 33126
(800) 443-9353

NEMA
National Electrical Manufacturers
 Association
2101 L Street N.W., Suite 300
Washington, DC 20037
(202) 457-8400

SAE (also covers aircraft engineers)
Society of Automotive Engineers
400 Commonwealth Drive
Warrendale, PA 15096-0001
(412) 776-4841

SME
Society of Manufacturing Engineers
One SME Drive
P.O. Box 930
Dearborn, MI 48121
(313) 271-1500

TWI
The Welding Institute
Abington Hall
Abington, Cambridge CB1 6AL
United Kingdom
(01) 0223-891162

INDEX